D1871347

THE
ANNEXATION OF THE PUNJAB,
AND THE
MAHARAJAH DULEEP SINGH

Owing to the antiquity and rarity of this book, certain pages are regrettably absent, and readability is compromised due to the blurring of the original text. If you possess any insights regarding the availability of these missing sections, kindly inform us. Your assistance is crucial in ensuring the completion of this significant work for the benefit of future generations.

THE ANNEXATION OF THE PUNJAB, AND THE MAHARAJAH DULEEP SINGH

MAJOR EVANS BELL

GYAN

Published by

GYAN

Gyan Publishing House
5, Ansari Road
Daryaganj, New Delhi-110002
Phone: 011-47034999, 9811692060
E-mail: books@gyanbooks.com

Distribution Network
gyanbooks.com
India, USA, Canada, UK, Australia

© Publisher

All rights reserved. No part of this work may be reproduced, stored, adapted, or transmitted in any form or by any means, electronic, mechanical, photocopying, micro-filming, recording or otherwise, or translated in any language, without the prior written permission of the copyright owner and the publisher.

ISBN: 978-93-6433-810-3 (HB)

First Published, 1882

2nd Impression 2024

Printed at: Gyan Press, Delhi.

The book is sold subject to the condition that it shall not, by way of trade or otherwise, be lent, resold, hired out, or otherwise circulated without the prior publisher's written consent.

THE ANNEXATION OF THE PUNJAB,
AND THE MAHARAJAH DULEEP SINGH
Author: MAJOR EVANS BELL

THE

ANNEXATION OF THE PUNJAUB,

AND THE

MAHARAJAH DULEEP SINGH.

BY

MAJOR EVANS BELL,

AUTHOR OF "LAST COUNSELS OF AN UNKNOWN COUNSELLOR", "THE OXUS AND THE INDUS"
"THE MYSORE REVERSION", ETC.

LONDON:

TRÜBNER & CO., LUDGATE HILL.

1882.

CONTENTS.

THE

MAHARAJAH DULEEP SINGH.

For the first time, it would appear, since the annexation of the Punjaub, the Maharajah Duleep Singh, in two letters addressed to the *Times*, dated the 28th of August and the 6th of September 1882*—the latter in reply to a leading article in the *Times* of the 31st of August,—has publicly expressed dissatisfaction with his treatment under the Terms which he was made to sign at Lahore, " for himself, his heirs and successors", on the 29th of March 1849.

Considering the Prince's long minority, his careful tutelage by gentlemen of the Anglo-Indian service, his English associations, and the amenities of his reception in society, it is not surprising that he has held his peace for such a long time, until, as it would seem, pressed by unexpected reverses and by natural anxieties for the future of his family.

The general belief in this country regarding the annexation of the Punjaub, and the provision made for the Maharajah Duleep Singh, is founded on what may be called an official myth or legend. The British Government, benevolently engaged in an endeavour to reform the administration of the Punjaub, is supposed to have been treacherously assailed by a general insurrection of

* Published in the *Times* of the 31st of August and 8th of September 1882.

"the Sikhs", and its generous intentions having thus been frustrated, and proved to be fruitless and hopeless, no practicable plan remained except that of annexing the country, which Lord Dalhousie carried out; and the Maharajah Duleep Singh, having been deprived of all claim to consideration by the bloodthirsty treason of his Ministers and followers, was treated with great forbearance, kindness and liberality, and endowed with a much larger income than could have been justly claimed for a Prince dethroned under such circumstances.

Historical truth differs very widely from this myth of official origin.

Many years have elapsed since, in reply to the Duke of Argyll,* Sir Charles Jackson,† Mr. J. C. Marshman, and other abettors and admirers of the iniquitous and injurious policy of annexation, I made what may be fairly called at this date an exhaustive and final exposure of the Marquis of Dalhousie's achievements, particularly of what was called "the conquest of the Punjaub".‡ The Duke of Argyll's little book was withdrawn from circulation, and since that time it may be said that no serious effort has been made to justify or defend Lord Dalhousie's various processes and principles of territorial acquisition.

Continuous and uniform experience, nowhere more conspicuous than in Oude, has utterly dissipated all the confident anticipations expressed by himself, his councillors and his school, as to financial gain for the Empire, and provincial prosperity for the people. Notwithstanding the limited and languid interest felt in Indian affairs, the verdict pronounced against Lord Dalhousie's policy

* *India under Dalhousie and Canning* (Longmans, 1865).

† *A Vindication of the Marquis of Dalhousie's Indian Administration* (Smith and Elder), 1865.

‡ *Retrospects and Prospects of Indian Policy* (Trübner), 1868.

by both the practical statesmanship and the popular sentiment of Great Britain, has never been reversed or shaken; and in obedience to the national fiat no renewal of acquisitive operations, except in the case of Mysore, which was negatived, has been proposed from Calcutta since the rebellion of 1857.

But although the political world at home may be pervaded by more healthy views and feelings, the old spirit of arrogant and grasping self-sufficiency, the spirit which informed and animated Lord Dalhousie as its instrument, still prevails among the Anglo-Indian "Services"—the alien bureaucracy domineering over a vast population, with no class of whom it mingles or sympathises. Nothing but a tempting opportunity is needed to bring us at any time from India some plausible proposal for annexing a State, for confiscating landed property, for mediatising a Prince, or for disendowing, wholly or in part, a Prince who has been mediatised. In the interests, therefore, of the Empire, the stability and solvency of which are undermined and endangered by every dereliction from treaty engagements and from Imperial good faith, I think it advisable that Chapter VI of my book, now out of print, containing the truth with regard to the Punjaub State and the Maharajah Duleep Singh, shall once more be placed before the public as an example and a warning.

The following pages will prove that, when the rebellion broke out in the Punjaub in 1848, the British Government was the Guardian of the Maharajah Duleep Singh. The exercise of the functions of Government in the Punjaub, the tutelage of the infant Sovereign, the custody of his Palace, his possessions and his person, remained for three years in the hands of the British Resident; and the quietude and continuity of that charge were never interrupted or disturbed for a single hour by any incident of the rebellion, or by any military operation in or near the capital city of Lahore. The British Government, under the guidance of Lord Dalhousie,—annexation being secretly premeditated,—turned the treaty of Guardianship to the fullest account, with the Maharajah's troops and resources, and the influence of his name, for the suppression of the rebellion, and then declared the Treaty to be at an end, and the Punjaub "conquered".

This will be enough to show that the Maharajah Duleep Singh did not in 1849, and does not now, stand before the British Government as an object of bounty, but as one who was in full and lawful possession of a sovereignty, with whom "Terms", equivalent to a Treaty of territorial cession, were concluded, which gave something like regularity and legality to what would otherwise have borne an aspect of naked lawlessness, and to what was, in fact, no "conquest", but a violent breach of trust.

ANNEXATION OF THE PUNJAUB.

THE Duke of Argyll says of the annexation of the Punjaub that "there is no need to defend it in point of right, and as little need now to support it in respect to policy."* Sir Charles Jackson considers that acquisition to be so completely removed from the sphere of controversy, that at the outset of the *Vindication* he declares his intention of "passing it over in silence." †

Mr. J. C. Marshman, formerly Editor of *The Friend of India*,‡ in his recently published History, declares, that "to offer any vindication of a measure which even the most prejudiced of Lord Dalhousie's opponents have not ventured to impugn, would be altogether redundant." § Those "fifth-rate writers"—as the Duke of Argyll calls them—are more "prejudiced" than Mr. Marshman supposes.

The annexation of the Punjaub was promptly impugned by Mr. John Sullivan, who had been a Member of Council at Madras, in a pamphlet published in 1850, and by Mr. J. M. Ludlow, in his "*British India, its Races and its History.*"‖ But, while I, also, must dispute both the right and the policy of that so-called conquest, I freely admit that,—mainly because it looked like a conquest,—

* *India under Dalhousie and Canning*, p. 4.

† *A Vindication*, p. 3.

‡ A weekly paper, published at Serampore near Calcutta, and conducted with great ability, which steadily supported all Lord Dalhousie's measures. Mr. Marshman is mentioned several times in General Sir William Sleeman's *Journey through Oude* (Bentley, 1858)—see vol. ii, pp. 390, 397,—as the writer of "rabid articles" in favour of the absorption of Native States; and is stigmatised by Sir Henry Lawrence as "a perfect filibuster",—Kaye's *Lives of Indian Officers*, vol. ii, p. 314. Any testimony, therefore, that we may extract from him will be understood as coming from a witness very favourable to Lord Dalhousie.

§ *History of India*. By John Clark Marshman (Longmans, 1867), vol. iii, p. 349.

‖ Vol. ii, pp. 166, 167.

it has never excited the same disgust as the annexations of Nagpore, Jhansi, and Oude. The iniquity of the transaction was shrouded by the smoke of battle ; and its impolicy, gradually becoming apparent, was hidden once more, for a time, when the Punjaub poured forth to our assistance, in the crisis of the rebellion, the troops that we had previously poured into it.

The same may be said of a still more iniquitous affair, the conquest of Scinde. There was a fight for it. Although the Ameers were goaded to resistance by a series of increasing demands, intolerable provocations, and a menacing advance upon their capital, the mere fact of their resistance made their violent expulsion from Scinde less injurious to our fame than the quiet spoliation of a friendly family. Public opinion in India, even in royal palaces, is not educated to the pitch of examining into the diplomatic details of a rupture, unless the scene of action be very close at hand. The sword was drawn ; blood was shed ; no further justification was required.

The impolicy of Lord Dalhousie's peaceful annexations consisted, in a great measure, in the moral aspect which they presented to the world of India. The moral objections to annexing the Punjaub were, doubtless, much less manifest. The impolicy was, therefore, less obvious. And I can well understand that Lord Dalhousie himself, when he decided on converting the Punjaub into a British Province, may have had few or none of those compunctious visitings, those "doubts and scruples", by which he was disturbed, according to the Duke of Argyll and Sir Charles Jackson, during the process of annexing Oude.*

In a despatch to the Secret Committee of the Court of Directors,—dated the 7th April 1849,—he endeavoured to prove that we could justly take advantage of our military force to make the Punjaub "a profitable possession"† for ourselves ; but the endeavour seems to me to be all in vain. No justification is made out at all.

Duleep Singh was the Ward of the British Government. Of this there can be no question. By the Articles of Agreement of the 16th December 1846, the British Go-

* *A Vindication*, p. 130 ; and *India under Dalhousie and Canning*, p. 69.

† *Papers, Punjaub*, 1849, p. 665.

vernment undertook "the maintenance of an administration, and the protection of the Maharajah Duleep Singh during the minority of his Highness."* This engagement was to "cease and terminate on his Highness attaining the full age of sixteen years, or on the 4th September 1854."† The Governor-General, Lord Hardinge, wished that "the new terms of agreement entered into for protecting the Maharajah during his minority, should be made as public as possible." In the General Proclamation of the 20th August 1847, the Governor-General announced that he felt "the interest of a father in the education and guardianship of the young Prince," and that "he had at heart the peace and security of this country", the Punjaub, "the firm establishment of the State, and the honour of the Maharajah and his Ministers."‡

In order "to maintain the administration of the Lahore State during the minority of the Maharajah," the Governor-General was armed with supreme and plenary power, and was "at liberty to occupy with British soldiers such positions as he may think fit, for the security of the capital, for the protection of the Maharajah, and the preservation of the peace of the country." The British Resident was placed at the head of the administration, with "full authority to direct and control all matters in every department of the State."§ Subject to the instructions of the Governor-General, "*unlimited powers*" were given to the Resident.‖

Lord Dalhousie declares that the British Government "maintained the Government of the State in the Council of Regency."¶ That Council was merely one part of the machinery instituted by the Governor-General, and kept in perfect subordination to British authority.

Lord Hardinge thus describes the new arrangement, in a despatch to the Secret Committee of the 21st December 1846.

* *Papers, Articles of Agreement with the Lahore Durbar*, 1847, p. 49.

† *Ibid.*, p. 51.

‡ *Papers, Punjaub*, 1849, p. 53.

§ *Papers, Articles of Agreement with the Lahore Durbar*, 1847, p. 50.

‖ *Papers, Punjaub*, 1849, pp. 35 and 48.

¶ *Ibid.*, 1849, p. 659.

"A Council of Regency, composed of leading Chiefs, will act under the control and guidance of the British Resident."

"The power of the Resident extends over every department, and to any extent."

"Those terms give the British Resident unlimited authority in all matters of internal administration, and external relations, during the Maharajah's minority."*

And in a letter dated the 3rd July 1847, the Governor-General reminds the Resident that the Articles of Agreement

"give to the Government of India, represented at Lahore by its Resident, full power to direct and control all matters in every department of the State."

"It is politic that the Resident should carry the Native Council with him, the members of which are, however, entirely under his control and guidance; he can change them and appoint others, and in military affairs his power is as unlimited as in the civil administration; he can withdraw Sikh garrisons, replacing them by British troops, in any and every part of the Punjab."†

The Resident himself, a month later, thus describes the working of the machine.

"On the whole, the Durbar" (the Council of Regency) "give me as much support as I can reasonably expect; there has been a quiet struggle for mastery, but as, though I am polite to all, I allow nothing that appears to me wrong to pass unnoticed, the members of the Council are gradually falling into the proper train, and refer most questions to me, and in words at least allow, more fully even than I wish, that they are only executive officers,—to do as they are bid."‡

Thus the Council of Regency never was "the Government of the State", as Lord Dalhousie calls it, without the British Resident at its head, to whom its members were strictly subordinate.

One important count in the indictment brought by Lord Dalhousie against "the Sikhs", is that whereas "they had bound themselves to submit to the full authority of the British Resident directing and controlling all matters in every department of the State,—*the Government of Lahore*, in reply to the orders of the

* *Papers, Articles of Agreement with the Lahore Durbar*, 1847, p. 24.

† *Papers, Punjaub*, 1849, p. 18. ‡ *Ibid.*, p. 32.

Resident, neither punished" the rebel Moolraj, when two British officers had been murdered at Mooltan, "nor gave reparation for the offence, but declared that their troops were not to be depended upon".* This attempt to separate the Resident from "the Government of Lahore", and to use the latter term as synonymous with "the Sikhs", is quite unwarrantable. The Resident was at the head of the Government of Lahore; the Councillors of Regency were merely "executive officers", "to do as they were bid", "under his control and guidance". "The Sikhs", however rebellious, were subjects, not responsible rulers. The Resident's "power" was "unlimited in military affairs". He could "withdraw Sikh garrisons, replacing them by British troops, in any and every part of the Punjaub". And when the military emergency arose, he pursued his own course by the tenor and spirit of these instructions, ordering the troops backwards and forwards, occasionally consulting the Durbar or informing them of his determinations, but never allowing them to adopt their own plans for restoring the peace of the country. The Resident was the Government of Lahore. When the news arrived of the outbreak at Mooltan, the Resident transferred none of his authority to the Councillors; he gave all the orders himself.

The first intelligence from Mooltan left the fate of the two British officers uncertain, and gave no particulars of what had passed. The Resident had decided on the 24th of April 1848, to support the Maharajah's force with a brigade of British troops. But when assured of the barbarous murder of the English officers, and the defection of their Sikh escort, the Resident countermanded the march of our brigade, because the Durbar troops might prove faithless.† After several false starts, and much vacillation, the British troops did not arrive before Mooltan until the 18th of August,‡ four months having elapsed since the outbreak.

During the continuance of this dangerous delay, several occurrences took place, eminently calculated to terrify, provoke, and exasperate the Sikh chieftains and army,

* *Papers, Punjaub*, 1849 p. 660.

† *Ibid.*, p. 139.

‡ *Ibid.*, p. 291.

and to drive them headlong into the rebellion of Dewan Moolraj, just when the splendid exploits of Lieutenant Edwardes (afterwards Colonel Sir Herbert Edwardes, K.C.B.) had made it appear almost hopeless. By the middle of July, Edwardes, with the Maharajah's troops, supported by the army of the Nawab of Bhawulpore, had defeated Moolraj in two pitched battles, and had forced the rebel leader to take refuge in his fortress. He had no army in the field; he was "hemmed in, disheartened by defeats, and weakened by desertions".* The news was spread throughout the Punjaub that a British force, with heavy guns, was on its way to destroy the great stronghold of revolt. The Resident was expecting to hear of Moolraj doing some "act of desperation" that would "close the rebellion",† when a fresh insurrection broke out, headed by Sirdar Chuttur Singh, the Nazim, or Governor, of the Hazara Province. On the 14th of September, Sirdar Chuttur Singh's son, Rajah Shere Singh, who was in command of a body of Durbar troops, co-operating with General Whish in the siege of Mooltan yielded at last to "his father's awful maledictions",‡ and the general disaffection of his Sikh officers and soldiers, and moved over to the enemy with his whole camp. Being much distrusted by the Dewan Moolraj, Shere Singh soon left Mooltan, and became the leader in a new rebellion, which assumed the most formidable dimensions. How can we account for this strange infatuation, reviving fanaticism in the breasts of those most interested in the preservation of peace and good order, and inciting them to revolt at the most inopportune moment, when their chance of success was desperate?

Three incidents mainly contributed to stimulate the second Sikh war,—the exile of the Maharanee, the refusal to fix a day for the Maharajah's marriage, and the treatment of Sirdar Chuttur Singh. The equity and expediency

* *Papers, Punjaub*, 1849, pp. 243, 250.

† *Ibid.*, p. 258. "My expectation is that the rebel will either destroy himself or be destroyed by his troops, before the next mail goes out." (June 22nd, 1848.) *Punjaub Papers*, 1849, p. 220.

‡ *A Year on the Punjaub Frontier*, by Major Edwardes, C.B., vol. ii, p. 446.

of all these measures may have seemed very defensible at the time, and may even now be asserted by those who took a part in them; but the question we have to consider is not so much whether each or all of these measures were wise and justifiable, as whether they were the work of the British Government, acting, under Treaty, as the Guardian and Trustee of the infant Sovereign. If the rebellion was aggravated and extended by the policy of British officers, approved and confirmed by the Governor-General, opposed and deprecated by the Council of Regency, the pretence of separating the Resident from "the Government of Lahore", and throwing off all responsibility from the autocratic head upon the consultative members, can no longer be maintained.

Of the Maharanee's bad intentions and incessant intrigues against the Council of Regency, there can be no doubt. But in her compulsory retirement at the country palace of Sheikhopoor, her evil influence was almost extinguished; and in May 1848, one of the most mischievous plots carried on in her name having been exposed and defeated, and the chief conspirators publicly executed, she would have been powerless, if left to her own devices. Two years after the annexation, Major Edwardes, who played such a brilliant part in these events, and had the best means of becoming acquainted with the facts, and with the weightiest opinions bearing upon them, writes that "the Ranee Jhunda, who had more wit and daring than any man of her nation, was weary of scattering 'ambiguous voices', and of writing incendiary epistles from Sheikhopoora to quondam *mauvais sujets.* Her memory survived, for she was not a woman to be forgotten; but her influence had followed her power, and there was no longer a man found in the Punjaub who would shoulder a musket at her bidding."*

It is perfectly clear that the strong measure of sending the Maharanee into banishment,—in fact imprisonment in exile,—was taken by the Resident, on his own judgment and authority, supported by the previously communicated permission of the Governor-General, but contrary

* *A Year on the Punjaub Frontier,* vol. ii, p. 412.

to the advice of the Council of Regency. The Resident, in a despatch dated the 16th May 1848, reports what had taken place on the preceding day.

"Maharanee Jhunda Khore, the mother of Maharajah Duleep Singh, was removed from the fort of Sheikhopoor, *by my orders*, yesterday afternoon; and is now on her way, under charge of an escort, to Ferozepore."

"Her summary banishment from the Punjaub, and residence at Benares, under the surveillance of the Governor-General's Agent, subject to such custody as will prevent all intrigue and correspondence for the future, *seems to me* the best course which we could adopt."*

There is not a word in the despatch to lead us to suppose that this step was approved by the Cabinet of Regency, or that they did anything more than act as "executive officers", and "do as they were bid." When relating any decision of importance, the Resident generally states that the Council "unanimously" agreed with him, or that they "yielded"; but in this case there is a significant silence on the subject of any discussion in Council.

We know that in August 1847, the Chiefs were "decidedly averse to incur what they considered the odium of participating in effecting the banishment of the Maharanee", and in consequence of their objections to sending her out of the country, her new residence was fixed at Sheikhopoor, only twenty miles from Lahore.†

The order for the Maharanee's removal and banishment is signed by only three of the Council of Regency, and of these only one, Rajah Tej Singh, the Ranee's bitter personal enemy, is a Sikh. The signature of Golab Singh, a mere youth and not a Councillor, is also attached, on behalf of his absent brother, Rajah Shere Singh, as if no means could be spared to fortify this document with the apparent concurrence of the Durbar.

And although it is signed by three members of the Council, and by the brother of a fourth, it only purports to be issued, "*according to the advice of Sir Frederick Currie, Bart., and Fakeer Noor-ood-deen*", a Mussulman

* *Papers, Punjaub*, 1849, p. 168.
† *Ibid.*, pp. 35 and 51.

Councillor, who, accompanied by two English officers, personally saw to the order being carried out.*

The Resident himself seems to have had some notion of the dangerous excitement that might be caused by this strong and severe measure. "A formal trial", he writes, "of Maharajah Runjeet Singh's widow would be most unpopular and hurtful to the feelings of the people."† Can he have really supposed that "the summary banishment" of Runjeet Singh's widow from her son's dominions would be less unpopular? But was there no alternative but a formal trial? Why should the Ranee not have been put on her defence, as she repeatedly demanded, in a private investigation? There may have been another reason for avoiding a formal or informal trial. The Resident says there is no doubt in his mind that the Maharanee was "deeply implicated" in "conspiracies for tampering with the sepoys, and making revolt and insurrection." But he adds:—"Legal proof of the delinquency of the Maharanee would not, perhaps, be obtainable."‡ She might have been acquitted.

The Resident, however, declares that "this is not a time for us to hesitate about doing what may appear necessary to punish state offenders, whatever may be their rank and station, and to vindicate the honour and position of the British Government".

"But," he continues, "while doing what we deem an act of justice and policy, it is not necessary or desirable to do it in a way to exasperate the feelings of the soldiery, and the Chiefs, or people. We must bear in mind that the Maharanee is the mother of the Sovereign, and the widow of our Ally, Maharajah Runjeet Singh; and we must respect the feelings which they entertain regarding the violation of the seclusion of females of high rank."

"I propose, *therefore*" (therefore!) "*that the Maharanee be sent to Benares under a strong guard;* that she be allowed to take with her her jewels, and such of her property as she may immediately require, and her domestic servants; and that she be accompanied by the venerable Fakeer Noor-ood-deen," a Mahomedan, "the personal

* *Papers, Punjaub*, 1849, p. 228. † *Ibid.*, p. 168. ‡ *Ibid.*

friend and adviser of the late Maharajah Runjeet Singh, and a person greatly respected by the Sikhs generally."

"At Benares," the Resident suggests, "she should be subject to such surveillance and custody," as will "prevent her having intercourse with parties beyond her own domestic establishment, and holding correspondence with any person, except through" the Governor-General's Agent, Major Macgregor.*

Not a hint was given to the Maharanee or her attendants, either in the Resident's note to her, or in the order from the Durbar, as to her destination. The deputation were expressly forbidden to "use any deceit" to induce her to come away quietly, but they were "to tell the Maharanee no more than was entered in the *purwanna*", or order.† In obedience to these instructions, Lieutenant Lumsden refused to satisfy her request for information as to "whither she was to be escorted".‡

"Happily," reports the Resident, "there was not the slightest opposition; all was acquiescence and civility, from the Maharanee downwards, *very probably somewhat induced by the executions which took place a few days ago.*"§

In a subsequent letter, the Resident observes that he had anticipated "*she would probably think she was doomed to the same fate as her confidential vakeel Moonshee Gunga Ram*",—who had been hanged a few days before. Therefore, by the Resident's permission, Lieutenant Lumsden assured her Highness, "*as the party left the fort*", that "she would be subjected to no injury or indignity".||

Thus was the mother of the Sovereign, and widow of our Ally, hurried away into exile, under imminent terror of immediate execution, in charge of two English officers and a Mahomedan Chief, escorted by a strong guard. This was the plan adopted by the British authorities to avoid exasperating the Sikh soldiery and people, or offending "the feelings which they entertain as to the violation of the seclusion of females of high rank"!!

By the 10th Article of the Treaty of 16th December 1846, the Maharanee was to receive an allowance of a lakh

* *Papers, Punjaub*, 1849, p. 169. † *Ibid.*, p. 229.
‡ *Ibid.*, p. 229. § *Ibid.*, p. 169. || *Ibid.*, p. 229.

and a half of rupees (£15,000) per annum. On her first removal from Lahore to Sheikhopoor, in August 1847, this stipend was reduced, in spite of the Treaty, to forty-eight thousand rupees (£4,800), and after her deportation to Benares to twelve thousand rupees (£1,200) a year. This second reduction was made in consideration of the fact that the Ranee was "taking with her a very large amount of private property and jewels".*

She was not allowed to remain in possession of her jewels and other "private property" very long. On the 30th June 1848, before her arrival at Benares, the Resident writes that a seizure has been made of important correspondence which, "if genuine, and it seems impossible it should be otherwise", proves, "beyond a shadow of doubt", the complicity of the Maharanee Jhunda Khore "in the late conspiracy, and in other intrigues and machinations". Among the important correspondence seized at Lahore were "some original letters *intended* for the Maharanee, *which were not delivered*, owing to her sudden removal",—very conclusive evidence!—and also "*some copies of letters addressed to her*"—still more conclusive! In order "to get hold of the originals of those last described", the Resident requests that "the greatest care may be taken to secure all her property and papers"; and that "*the Maharanee should even be subjected to have her person, and those of her confidential slave women, searched* by respectable females, appointed for that purpose by the Governor-General's Agent".†

The news of these little courtesies, so eminently calculated to soothe the exasperated feelings of the Sikh Chieftains and soldiery, so congenial to their uncivilised notions of the respect due to "the seclusion of ladies of high rank", may possibly have created somewhat of a sensation when spread through the Punjaub.

The Resident further suggested that "the confinement of the Maharanee, on reaching Benares, should be much more stringent than was at first intended", and that "as a state prisoner, she should not be allowed to have the command of wealth, of which she has, hitherto, not scrupled to make use to accomplish purposes the most

* *Papers, Punjaub*, 1849, pp. 179 and 577. † *Ibid.*, p. 235.

treasonable, and to procure open violence and murder, and secret assassination."*

The Resident's suggestions were carried out; the Ranee's papers were all secured, but nothing treasonable, or of any importance, was found.† She was also deprived of all her jewels and valuables.‡

The effect of the Maharanee's deportation upon the Sikh soldiery was *instantaneous.* The Resident himself writes as follows to the Governor-General on the 25th May 1848.

"The reports from Rajah Shere Singh's camp are, that the Khalsa soldiery, on hearing of the removal of the Maharanee, were much disturbed; they said that she was the Mother of the Khalsa, and that, as she was gone, and the young Duleep Singh in our hands, they had no longer any one to fight for or uphold; that they had no inducement to oppose Moolraj: and if he came to attack them, would seize the Sirdars and their officers, and go over to him."§

A prominent place is given to this cause of general disgust and indignation in Shere Singh's Manifesto.

"It is well known to all the inhabitants of the Punjaub, to the whole of the Sikhs, and in fact to the world at large, with what oppression, tyranny and undue violence, the Feringhees have treated the widow of the great Maharajah Runjeet Singh, now in bliss."

"They have broken the Treaty by imprisoning, and sending away to Hindostan, the Maharanee, the Mother of her people."||

Dost Mahomed the Ruler of Cabool, in his letter to Captain Abbott, alleges this grievance as the chief cause of disaffection in the Punjaub.

"There can be no doubt that the Sikhs are daily becoming more and more discontented. Some have been dismissed from service, while others have been banished to Hindostan, in particular the mother of Maharajah Duleep Singh, who has been

* *Ibid.*, pp. 235, 236. † *Papers, Punjaub*, 1849, pp. 263, 266.

‡ *Ibid.*, pp. 263, 575. It may be added that the Maharanee was afterwards removed, for greater security, to the fortress of Chunar, but in a very few days after her arrival there she escaped in disguise, on the 18th of April 1849, and took refuge in Nepaul. In 1863 she came to England to visit her son, the Maharajah Duleep Singh, and died in this country that year.

§ *Ibid.*, p. 179. || *Ibid.*, p. 362.

imprisoned and ill-treated. Such treatment is considered objectionable by all creeds, and both high and low prefer death."*

There can be little doubt as to the Maharanee's incessant and malicious intrigues after her first removal to Sheikhopoor, and the reduction of the income guaranteed to her by the Treaty. That she would have had no scruple in getting her great enemy Rajah Tej Singh's throat cut if she could, and in damaging or disgracing one or two other members of the Regency, may well be believed. It was only to be expected that every one who engaged in rebellion or conspiracy, should make a free use of her name, and profess to act on her behalf. and with her sanction. But she is represented on all hands as a remarakbly clever woman, and it appears highly improbable that she should have been so blind to British power, so forgetful of recent lessons, so regardless of her son's interests, upon which her own future position entirely depended, as to provoke, with a divided country and diminished resources, another struggle between the Khalsa and the Company. It is utterly incredible. Not only is there no "legal proof", as the Resident admits, but there is nothing to be found in the Blue Book which amounts to substantial evidence, or affords any moral grounds for concluding that she ever compassed or countenanced such a renewed struggle, before her removal to Benares. In exile and degradation, stripped of her jewels, cash, and other property, deprived of her papers, forbidden to have an interview with any one, even with an English attorney, except in the presence of the Governor-General's Agent,† she may very probably have plunged into desperate plots of revenge, and opened a secret communication with the leading insurgents.

The deportation and imprisonment of the Maharanee, declared by Lord Dalhousie to have been intended not only as a "precaution", but as a "punishment",‡ appears to me to have been a measure as impolitic as it was unjudicial. Whatever that lady's crimes and conspiracies may have been,—and we have nothing to prove them but a mass of vituperative assertions,—it might have been

* *Papers, Punjaub*, 1849, p. 512. † *Ibid.*, 1849, p. 575.
‡ *Ibid.*, pp. 575, 578.

foreseen, and, doubtless, was foreseen and predicted by the Council of Regency, that her persecution would be ten times more provocative to the Sikhs, and more injurious to British honour and authority, than her continued intrigues could possibly have been.

The Ranee's banishment was looked upon by all who were attached to Runjeet Singh's kingdom, at once as a national insult, and as a preliminary step to the dethronement of her son, and the destruction of the State.

Rajah Shere Singh was one of those "Chiefs of the greatest note", whom, having first despatched towards Mooltan with all the disposable troops of the Sikh Army, the Resident recalled to receive the ominous injunction and warning that they must "put down the rebellion by their own means, as the only hope of saving their Government."* It was in his camp, as we have just seen, that the alarm and excitement first rose, when the Maharanee's deportation from the Punjaub became known.

But Shere Singh had not only the disaffection of his own troops to contend with. A storm was brewing in another quarter. His father, Sirdar Chuttur Singh, the Nazim or Governor of the Hazara Province, began to be involved, in the month of July, in certain personal difficulties, to be described hereafter, which led him to fear that his own ruin, and that of Runjeet Singh's kingdom, were objects predetermined by the British authorities. The old Sirdar kept up a regular correspondence with his son, Rajah Shere Singh, in the Camp at Mooltan, and with his younger son, Golab Singh, at Lahore. He was probably, in common with the Sikhs in general, somewhat alarmed and disgusted by the Maharanee's exile, and other menacing incidents and rumours: and when his anxieties were redoubled by the dangers impending over himself, he thought of applying a test to the secret intentions of the British Government, to ascertain whether the Treaty was to be broken,—whether the outrages and rebellion of Mooltan were to be visited on the innocent Duleep Singh. The youthful Maharajah was betrothed to Sirdar Chuttur Singh's daughter,—Rajah Shere Singh's sister. The Resident should be

* *Papers, Punjaub*, 1849, pp. 137, 140.

asked to fix a day for the marriage to take place. If he consented, it would be a sign of continued friendship, and good faith: if there were any evasion or hesitation, it would be a proof of some sinister purpose. Major Edwardes writes as follows to the Resident on the 28th July 1848:—

"Yesterday evening Rajah Shere Singh Attareewalla begged me to grant him a private interview, at which he laid before me the wishes of his father, Sirdar Chuttur Singh.

"If it is not your intention that the nuptials of the Maharajah should be celebrated some time within the next twelve months, the Sirdar would wish to be allowed to lay aside the duties of his Hazara Government, and proceed on pilgrimage for two years; if, on the contrary, the marriage is to take place this year, the Sirdar would suggest that, with your sanction, the Durbar should appoint astrologers, on the part of the Maharajah, to fix an auspicious month and day, in conjunction with other astrologers on the part of the bride.

"The above is the substance of the Rajah's conversation; and he earnestly requested me to procure him an answer from you within ten days. The request seems strange at the present moment. The secret motives of men are difficult to divine; but there can be no question that an opinion has gone very prevalently abroad, and been carefully disseminated by the evil disposed, that the British meditate declaring the Punjaub forfeited by the recent troubles and misconduct of the troops; and whether the Attareewalla family have any doubts, or not, upon this point themselves, it would, I think, be a wise and timely measure to give such public assurance of British good faith, and intention to adhere to the Treaty, as would be involved in authoritative preparations for providing the young Maharajah with a Queen. It would, no doubt, settle men's minds greatly."*

The Resident returned a very stiff official reply to this application, carefully avoiding any such "assurance", public or private, as Rajah Shere Singh wished to elicit, though endeavouring to satisfy him with common-place courtesies. He observes that "all the ceremonies for affiancing being complete, it would, in common usage, rest with the family of the bride to determine the time when the actual ceremony of marriage should take place"; but that "of course, with reference to the position of the Maharajah, *nothing can be done in this case without the concurrence and appro-*

* *Papers, Punjaub*, 1849, pp. 270, 271.

bation of the Resident." He will "consult, confidentially, the members of the Durbar now at Lahore on the subject of the time at which the marriage should be celebrated", and Rajah Shere Singh may be assured that the British Government will only interfere "to secure that all is done which may be best calculated to promote the honour and happiness of the Maharajah, and of the bride and her family."

And then come these portentous words;—"I do not see how the proceeding with the ceremonies for the Maharajah's nuptials *can be considered as indicative of any line of policy which the Government may consider it right to pursue now, or at any future time, in respect to the administration of the Punjaub*, and it is, on that account, that I see no objection to the marriage being celebrated at such time, and in such manner, as may be most satisfactory to the parties themselves, and the Durbar."*

Major Edwardes can now have had no doubt as to the views in favour at Head-quarters; and, however cautiously he may have communicated to Shere Singh the substance of the Resident's answer, the Rajah and his father must have felt henceforth but little hope that the Sovereignty of Duleep Singh would be allowed to survive the suppression of the actual revolt. The less Major Edwardes said on the subject, the more they must have been alarmed.

Major Edwardes says: "Unhappily the full meaning of the application did not appear."† It must have appeared clearly enough to the Resident by the light of Major Edwardes's own lucid explanation, which we have just quoted. The cold and studied reply indicates that the question was fully understood. And by the aid of their other informants at Lahore, where Rajah Shere Singh's brother, Golab Singh, had access to the Resident, we may be sure that the full meaning of the reply to their urgent application was understood by the two Sikh Chieftains. The Resident would not admit that the Maharajah's marriage was a matter of political signifi-

* *Papers, Punjaub*, 1849, pp. 272, 273.

† *A Year on the Punjaub Frontier*, vol. ii, p. 448.

cance, or public consequence; and he would not promise to take any immediate steps to have a day fixed for its celebration. "Of course, nothing can be done without the concurrence and approbation of the Resident", but "he will consult the Durbar confidentially."

Just at the time when Sirdar Chuttur Singh must have received the news from his sons of the negative result of his test, he was himself falling into great straits.

Sirdar Chuttur Singh was the Nazim, or Governor, of the Hazara Province, inhabited by an armed Mahomedan population,—"warlike and difficult of control",*—who entertained a bitter and bigoted hostility to all who bore the name of Sikh. Under Runjeet Singh's Government the Province had never been effectually settled, and the revenues were only occasionally collected by a military expedition. Captain James Abbott, one of the Resident's Assistants,† was appointed to aid and advise the Sikh Governor in the execution of his duties. Very soon after the outbreak under Dewan Moolraj at Mooltan, Captain Abbott became impressed with the belief that Chuttur Singh was "at the head of a conspiracy for the expulsion of the English from the Punjaub, and was about to head a crusade against the British forces at Lahore."‡ From that time Captain Abbott took up his abode at a place thirty-five miles distant from Chuttur Singh's residence,§ and "shut himself out from all personal communication" with his colleague.‖ "The constant suspicion", writes the Resident, "with which Captain Abbott regarded Sirdar Chuttur Singh, seems to have, not unnaturally, estranged that Chief from him."¶

The Blue Book affords ample materials for balancing the antecedent probabilities in this case. Nearly a year before his differences with Chuttur Singh commenced, the Resident, Sir Henry Lawrence, had written of Captain Abbott to the Governor-General in these terms:—"Captain Abbott is an excellent officer; but he is too apt to

* *Papers, Punjaub*, 1849, p. 18.

† Distinguished before that period for his enterprising journey to Khiva, well described by his own pen, now a General and C.B.

‡ *Papers, Punjaub*, 1849, p. 279. § *Ibid.*, p. 279.

‖ *Ibid.*, p. 285. ¶ *Ibid.*, p. 279.

take gloomy views of questions. I think he has unwittingly done Dewan Jowala Sahaee injustice." Of this Dewan Jowala Sahaee Sir Henry Lawrence adds, "I only know one better Native. According to the light he has enjoyed, the times he has lived in, and the school in which he has been brought up, he is a respectable, as he is assuredly an able, man."*

On a later occasion, the succeeding Resident, Sir Frederick Currie, shows us Captain Abbott falling into the same hasty and unfounded suspicions of another Sikh Chief, Jhunda Singh.

"Soon after the defection of a portion of the Churrunjeet Regiment of Horse, which formed a part of Sirdar Jhunda Singh's Brigade (on which occasion the Sirdar's conduct was open to no sort of suspicion), Captain Abbott wrote of Jhunda Singh as one connected with the extensive band of conspirators whom he considered as leagued to aid the Mooltan rebellion.

"Upon that occasion I explained to Captain Abbott, that if his opinion of Sirdar Jhunda Singh's disaffection rested on the facts he had mentioned, it was without due foundation; for that the Sirdar had closely and scrupulously obeyed my orders in every step he had taken."†

Besides these two particular instances of Captain Abbott's special infirmity, we find in the Blue Book the Resident's judgment on that officer's general capacity as a political detective, professing to observe the obscure symptoms of a nascent insurrection.

"His Lordship will have observed a very ready disposition on the part of Captain Abbott to believe the reports that are brought to him of conspiracies, treasons, and plots, suspicion of everybody, far and near, even of his own servants, and a conviction of the infallibility of his own conclusions, which is not shaken by finding time after time that they are not verified."‡

Who, on the other hand, was Sirdar Chuttur Singh, so unfortunately associated with this perverse coadjutor? The Resident tells us that he was "an old and infirm man, the father-in-law of the Maharajah, with more at stake than almost any man in the Punjaub".§

"Sirdar Chuttur Singh is a wily old Chief of Runjeet Singh's time, who has been concerned in his day in many treacherous pro-

* *Papers, Punjaub*, p. 30.
† *Ibid.*, 1849, p. 328.
‡ *Ibid.*, p. 285.
§ *Ibid.*, p. 279.

ceedings, and is the confidential friend of Maharajah Golab Singh; but he is now infirm and in ill health, and has obtained much wealth, and an honourable position in the present administration, while his daughter is the betrothed wife of the young Maharajah of Lahore."*

"Mr. John Lawrence, in a private letter received yesterday, writing of him, says, 'I cannot, in any way, account for Chuttur Singh's conduct; I always looked on him as a harmless old fool. He is, moreover, now very infirm, and suffers much from chronic disease."†

In another despatch he observes:—"Sirdar Chuttur Singh and his sons were raised to their present position by the arrangements of Lieutenant-Colonel Lawrence, with the approbation of the British Government. The family is unpopular with the Chiefs and the old adherents of Runjeet Singh, as being upstarts, and the creatures of the British Government. They are unpopular with the army, * * * and they have no weight with the people."‡

In the midst of the agitation caused throughout the Punjaub by the delay and uncertainty following the first successes of Major Edwardes against the Dewan Moolraj, Captain Abbott received intelligence, upon which he placed reliance, that the Brigade of Durbar troops stationed at Pukli, near the residence of Sirdar Chuttur Singh, had determined on marching either to Mooltan or to Lahore, to join in the insurrection. So far as can be gathered from the Blue Book, his information showed that a portion of the force was in an excited and disaffected state; but Captain Abbott himself reports that the officers "did not countenance the men in the move", that they "made a show of putting down the mutiny", and that they fired "two successive salutes", in honour of the "two victories of Lieutenant Edwardes". He also states that the Golundauz or Artillerymen, and the Zumboorchees, or camel-gunners, were "disinclined to the move".§ Thus the disaffection, by his own account, was by no means general or decided. Nothing whatever appears to prove that Sirdar Chuttur Singh promoted or approved the misconduct of the evil-disposed among the Sikh troops.

* *Papers, Punjaub*, 1849, p. 286.

† *Ibid.*, p. 334.

‡ *Ibid.*, p. 380.

§ *Ibid.*, p. 310.

Captain Abbott, however, had satisfied himself that Chuttur Singh was at the head of a vast conspiracy, and was about to march upon Lahore at the head of all the Durbar troops in Hazara. During the first week of August 1848, without any warning, without any communication with the Governor of the Province, Sirdar Chuttur Singh, without any intimation to his own official superiors, Captain Abbott roused the armed Mahomedan peasantry, over whom he had obtained great influence, and closed the passes by which the Brigade stationed at Pukli could descend into the plains. On the 6th of August "the mountaineers assembled in great numbers, and surrounded the town of Hurripore", where Sirdar Chuttur Singh was residing. The Sirdar was induced, as a natural movement of self-defence, to order the detachment of troops, which was stationed for the protection of the town, to encamp on the esplanade under the guns of the fort.* Colonel Canora, an American, who had been for some years in the Sikh service, refused to move out of the city to the new position with the battery of Artillery under his command, unless by Captain Abbott's permission. Sirdar Chuttur Singh "repeated his orders, saying that Captain Abbott could not know the peril they were in from the threatened attack of the armed population, who could easily seize the guns where they were".† Canora not only refused to obey these orders, but loaded two of his guns with double charges of grape, and "standing between them with a lighted portfire in his hand, said he would fire upon the first man who came near".‡ Sirdar Chuttur Singh sent two companies of Sikh Infantry to take possession of the guns. Colonel Canora first cut down one of his own Havildars, or Sergeants, who had refused to fire upon the Infantry, and then applied the match himself to one of the guns, which missed fire. At that moment he was struck down by musket shots from two of the Infantry soldiers. After his fall, and before he expired, he is said to have killed two Sikh officers with his double barrelled pistol.§

* *Papers, Punjaub*, 1849, p. 279.
† *Ibid.*, p. 280.
‡ *Ibid.*, pp. 287 and 303.
§ *Ibid.*, pp. 280, 301, 303.

Captain Abbott calls this most justifiable and unavoidable homicide, "an atrocious deed", "a cold-blooded murder, as base and cowardly as that of Peshora Singh",* and talks about Chuttur Singh having "*determined* upon the murder" of Colonel Canora.†

The Resident, in several letters to Captain Abbott, having received both his account of the affair and that of Sirdar Chuttur Singh makes the following sound and sensible observations:—

"The death of Commedan Canora is stated, both by the Sirdar and yourself, to have been occasioned in consequence of his disobedience of the reiterated orders of the Nazim, and his having offered violent opposition to those whom the Governor, after many remonstrances with the Commedan, sent to enforce his orders.

"I cannot at all agree with you as to the character you assign to this transaction. Sirdar Chuttur Singh was the Governor of the province, military and civil, and the officers of the Sikh army were bound to obey him, the responsibility for his orders resting with him. Taking the worst possible view of the case, I know not how you can characterise it as 'a cold-blooded murder, as base and cowardly as that of Peshora Singh.'‡

"It is clear that whatever may have been the intention of the Pukli Brigade, no overt act of rebellion was committed by them till the initiative was taken by you, by calling out the armed peasantry and surrounding the Brigade in its cantonment. It seems, also, that the armed peasants were threatening Hurripore, before the Nazim ordered the guns out of the town, to the open space between the fort and the city.

"I have given you no authority to raise levies, and organise paid bands of soldiers, to meet an emergency, of the occurrence of which I have always been somewhat sceptical.

"It is much, I think, to be lamented that you have kept the Nazim at a distance from you; have resisted his offers and suggestions to be allowed himself to reside near you, or to have his son, Ootar Singh, to represent him at Shirwan; and that you have judged of the purposes, and feelings and fidelity of the Nazim

---

* *Papers, Punjaub*, p. 302. Peshora Singh, one of several pretenders to the throne of the Punjaub, was in open rebellion against the Lahore Government in March 1845, when he was captured by the troops under Chuttur Singh, and put to death in prison by order of the Minister, Jowahir Singh, the Maharanee's brother. Chuttur Singh does not seem to have been to blame.—Trotter's *History of India* from 1844 to 1862, vol. i, p. 42.

† *Idem*, p. 311.

‡ *Papers, Punjaub*, 1849, p. 313.

and the troops, from the reports of spies and informers, very probably interested in misrepresenting the real state of affairs.

"None of the accounts that have yet been made justifies you in calling the death of Commedan Canora a murder, nor in asserting that it was premeditated by Sirdar Chuttur Singh. That matter has yet to be investigated."*

Chuttur Singh was eventually goaded into open rebellion. Captain Abbott having predicted his treason, took, with perfect good faith, the best measures to prove his prediction true. Having played an aggressive part, and forced Chuttur Singh "to take his line",† Captain Abbott acted with ability and energy; and though he could not accomplish the task he had assigned himself, that of destroying the Sikh troops by means of the Mahomedan mountaineers, he maintained a defensive position in Hazara till the end of the war. When Chuttur Singh had committed himself beyond retreat by a series of acts of contumacy and hostility, Captain Abbott's provocative policy was glossed over and consigned to oblivion. But there is nothing whatever in the Blue Book to show that the Resident ever saw reason to withdraw or modify his opinion that "the initiative was taken" by Captain Abbott. The insurrection in Hazara was, in fact, originally an insurrection of the Mahomedan peasantry, with the object of exterminating the Sikh troops and Governor, instigated and promoted by a British officer.‡

It is interesting to observe the spirit in which Captain Abbot devised and prosecuted his offensive operations. It goes very far to explain the powerful influence which he obtained over the fanatical Mahomedans of the Hazara Hills. Besides money, he gave them what they most coveted, an opportunity of revenge and triumph over the

* *Papers, Punjaub*, 1849, p. 316. † *Ibid.*, p. 323.

‡ It is worthy of note that, at the end of the campaign, "Abbott alone, who had held his lonely post at Nara from first to last, was unfairly stinted of the honours due to his acknowledged worth," when Edwardes, Lake, Taylor and Herbert were decorated and promoted.—Trotter's *History of India from* 1844 *to* 1862, vol. i, p. 212. "The gallant Abbott, who had defended the fortress of Nara against fearful odds, down to the close of the campaign, was invidiously refused the honour due to his distinguished efforts and success."—Marshman's *History of India* (Longmans, 1867), vol. iii, p. 350. *Somebody* appreciated his services justly, if Lord Dalhousie did not.

idolatrous Sikhs, the obstinate persecutors of the Mussulman faith. I quote from Captain Abbott's own despatches.

"I assembled the Chiefs of Hazara; explained what had happened, and called upon them by the memory of their murdered parents, friends and relatives, to rise, and aid me in destroying the Sikh forces in detail. I issued *purwannas* to this effect throughout the land, and marched to a strong position."*

"I have placed a force in the Margulla Pass to destroy Pertaub Singh's Regiment, should it refuse to turn back at my reiterated orders."†

"I have ordered out the armed peasantry, and will do my best to destroy the Sikh army."‡

"The Sirdar sent me no intelligence of this cold-blooded murder, as base and cowardly as his murder of Peshora Singh, but on finding it confirmed by eye-witnesses, and that the Sirdar had thus identified himself with the mutineers in Pukli, I ordered all the Chiefs of Hazara to rise, and, in every way, harass and molest those who should support him."§

It must be mentioned that there were no "mutineers in Pukli"; Captain Abbott had no information of anything like a mutiny; he was acting merely on the rumours of a secret conspiracy, brought or written to him, from a distance of thirty-five miles, by spies and informers. No overt act had been committed before his own hostile movements. His own letters prove that before the unfortunate Canora's death, there was nothing apparent or even alleged against Sirdar Chuttur Singh that required investigation. He presses matters on to a climax.

"I left Shirwan for a position nearer the new theatre of operations, the foot of the Gundgurk mountains,—terrible to the Sikhs for three most bloody and disastrous defeats, from numbers not one-fourth of their own. It is within sight of Hurripore, and may be called the throne of Hazara, as here I have at my back the bravest and most loyal of the population, and my orders are better obeyed than from any other locality."‖

From this "throne", he sent to Hurripore, and summoned Chuttur Singh to give up "the murderers", as he called them, of Colonel Canora, and to comply with "a schedule of demands".

* *Papers, Punjaub*, 1849, p. 311. † *Ibid.*, p. 306.
‡ *Ibid.*, p. 301. § *Ibid.*, p. 302. ‖ *Ibid.*, p. 303.

"I have given him until to-morrow morning for decision. If he then refuse the terms, I shall be satisfied that it is not mere alarm about himself from the population of Hazara, but a sense of detected guilt, and consequent desperation, which has led to this rebellious conduct. If he comply, *the country need not be ravaged, nor the army destroyed,* and his conduct may be made the subject of legal investigation.

"The Pukli Brigade is still in limbo. It is unfortunate that the Pukli Brigade got intelligence of my possession of that pass in time, *as, in all probability it would have been destroyed.* As it never actually marched, I am reluctant to order it to be destroyed, until in motion."*

Here is another distinct admission, out of his own mouth, that no overt act had been committed. It was, in his own opinion, "unfortunate", that these obstinate Sikhs would not mutiny, or march to Lahore, in time. He was "reluctant" to have them "destroyed" in their quarters, because they had not moved. Yet he had already ordered the armed peasantry to "destroy the Sikh army", and "to harass and molest, in every way", those who supported the Governor of the Province.

In another place Captain Abbott declares that the "murder" of Canora "formed the break in the ice of *deep and silent treachery, so long carried on with a smiling face*",†—acknowledging, in fact, that, before that unhappy event, he had nothing to bring against Chuttur Singh except vague rumours of conspiracy. As the Resident wrote to him:—"There is no proof of misconduct before the raising of the armed population, and his plea is, that all that he has done since, has been of a defensive character."‡

More than once Captain Abbott betrays his consciousness that he had given Chuttur Singh good cause for alarm, and for the precautionary measures which were bringing them into collision. "I wrote to the Sirdar," he says, "insisting upon the instant surrender of the murderers of this loyal and gallant officer, and the return of the troops to their cantonments, promising, upon these conditions, *to settle all disturbances in the country*",§—a pretty plain admission that the disturbances in Hazara were all of his own making.

* *Papers, Punjaub*, 1849, p. 303.
† *Ibid.*, p. 311.
‡ *Ibid.*, p. 313.
§ *Ibid.*, p. 302.

"He" (Chuttur Singh) "says that Canora was engaged to join the peasants in plundering Hurripore. He"—evidently Canora—"knew nothing whatever of what was passing amongst the people of the country, *and more than once expressed anxiety lest the town should be plundered.**

"If the murderers of Colonel Canora are surrendered to me for judgment, and the troops sent back to their several cantonments, *I will, instantly, reduce the country to its former profound tranquillity.*"†

There is an occasional inconsistency, amounting almost to incoherence, running through Captain Abbott's reports, in spite of his bold and confident doings. For instance, after declaring his intention of "destroying the Sikh army in detail", and "harassing and molesting" everyone who should support the Governor, he complains of that personage having expressed alarm at the rising of the armed peasantry, and having written in "a tone of virtuous indignation", under a "pretence of extreme peril from a people *whom two of my chuprassees*" (messengers) "*would settle in three days*".‡ As if it were very likely that either the Mahomedan population on the one side, roused by appeals to their "murdered parents", and to the "bloody defeats" they had formerly inflicted on the Sikhs";§ or the Sikh Governor and troops, on the other, alarmed by the sudden insurrection, would interpret Captain Abbott's exterminating orders and proclamations with all that moderation and reluctance, and all those conditions and qualifications, with which he professes to have tempered them!

The Resident had too much good sense and experience to look upon the calling up of these fanatical mountaineers as a mere demonstration, which Captain Abbott could easily keep in hand, and settle at any moment with "two of his *chuprassees*". He very properly calls it "a momentous business", and tells the Governor-General, "I have pointed out to him how much easier it is to raise, than to allay a power thus brought into action, and impelled by religious antipathies, and feelings of long-cherished hatred".‖

The Resident writes to Captain Abbott that both of

* *Papers, Punjaub*, 1849, p. 303. † *Ibid.*, p. 304.
‡ *Ibid.*, p. 304. § *Ante*, p. 119. ‖ *Papers, Punjaub*, p. 279.

Sirdar Chuttur Singh's sons, Rajah Shere Singh, at Mooltan, and Golab Singh, at Lahore, complain that their father has been "betrayed into misconduct by mistrust, engendered by your withdrawal of your confidence from him, and declared suspicions of his fidelity, and by fear at the Mahomedan population having been raised, as he believed, for his destruction and that of the Sikh army."*

What Chuttur Singh believed, was the exact truth. Captain Abbott himself tells us so repeatedly. He speaks of "arousing a high-spirited people to the work of destruction."† The Mahomedan population was raised by him "to destroy the Sikh army", and to "harass and molest" everyone who should support the Sikh Governor.

The Resident on the 19th August 1848, writes to Captain (afterwards General) John Nicholson, who, under his instructions, was endeavouring to arrange matters, and bring all parties to their bearings, as follows :—

"We must bear in mind that, whatever may have been supposed to have been the purpose of the Pukli Brigade and the Sirdar, no overt act was committed by either until the Brigade was surrounded in Gahundia, and Hurripore was threatened by the Mahomedan tribes, of whose purpose no notice had been given by Captain Abbott to Sirdar Chuttur Singh, the Governor of the Province. The initiative was clearly taken by Captain Abbott,—I do not say unnecessarily, but it was so taken; and the Nazim now pleads that he was acting for the protection of himself and the troops committed to him, and also of the country under his government, in calling the regiments from Hassan Abdal and the other cantonments."‡

Captain Nicholson writes back to the same effect, and suggests "a full pardon to the Sirdar for all that has occurred."§

At this time, and even on previous dates, Captain Abbott's inflammatory language exaggerates and misrepresents what he calls the "crimes" of Chuttur Singh. He writes to the Resident, on the 13th August, that Chuttur Singh is "exciting to mutiny the bulk of the Sikh army, and calling upon the Jummoo Prince" (the Rajah of Cashmere) "to invade the country." "Last

* *Papers, Punjaub,*, 1849, p. 296.
† *Ibid.*, p. 309.
‡ *Ibid.*, p. 312.
§ *Ibid.*, pp. 308, 309.

night I intercepted letters from Sirdar Chuttur Singh to Maharajah Golab Singh" (of Cashmere), "the Rajahs Jowahir Singh and Runbeer Singh" (Golab Singh's nephew and son), "and others, entreating the aid of four Jummoo Regiments."*

What he calls "exciting the Sikh army to mutiny", was, as admitted by the Resident and Captain Nicholson, sending for the Regiments from the neighbouring cantonments for the protection of himself and the troops against the insurgent Mahomedans. As for the intercepted letters, they are the best evidence of the Sirdar's innocence at that period, for, containing no treasonable matter, or Captain Abbott would have been sure to mention it, and being couched, as he says, "in a tone of virtuous indignation", they, also, were simply appeals for aid, written under the influence, as Captain Nicholson said, of "terror and anxiety."†

When the news of Chuttur Singh's movements first reached Mooltan, his son, Rajah Shere Singh "discussed the matter with me", said Major Edwardes, to whom Shere Singh showed the letters received from his father, "with great good sense, and put it to me, whether all that his father had done to oppose the Moolkias" (the insurgent peasantry) "was not perfectly natural and excusable, on the supposition that he was innocent of the plots suspected by Captain Abbott. 'No man', he said, 'will allow himself to be killed without a struggle.'"‡

The insurmountable obstacle, as Captain Nicholson at once perceived, was the death of Colonel Canora, and the requisition for the men who shot him. Chuttur Singh had rewarded these men on the spot, a very natural proceeding in his position and with his notions, but which, he felt, fixed upon him the stigma of the murder, if such it was to be considered by the English authorities. "He has identified himself with the murderers in paying them for their bloody work", wrote Captain Abbott to the Resident.§ It is perfectly obvious that if Chuttur Singh had taken a step towards giving up those men to what they and their comrades

* *Papers, Punjaub*, 1849, p. 304.
† *Ibid.*, p. 308.
‡ *Ibid.*, p. 294.
§ *Ibid.*, p. 311.

would have supposed to be certain death, he would not merely have sacrificed his own honour uselessly, —for there was no secret about his having rewarded them,—but it would in all probability have brought on an immediate mutiny, to which he would himself have fallen the first victim.

The Resident seems to have had a general idea that the principal difficulty of the case was concentrated on this point. "After the death of Canora", he writes to the Government, "the Sirdar thought himself compromised irretrievably, it would appear, with us."*

Major (now General Sir) George Lawrence, also writes:—"He" (Chuttur Singh) "is anxious to come to terms, but fears he has committed himself too far to admit of his obtaining them."†

We are not surprised to find that he could obtain no terms from Captain Abbott. That officer refused to see Chuttur Singh, who offered to wait upon him, if assured of a free pardon. "I declined this; thought it quite impossible that we should meet amicably, until I knew the sentiments of Government upon his conduct."‡

"I gave him yesterday", writes Captain Abbott to the Resident, "a statement of my demands, viz., the surrender of the murderers for judgment, and an order to the several Regiments to return to their duty."§

But from the Resident we might have expected a more even-handed procedure, and a more impartial arbitrament. Satisfied that the death of Canora, even according to Captain Abbott's version, was not a murder, he might surely have dealt more judiciously with that "insurmountable obstacle", the peremptory demand for the surrender of "the murderers" into Captain Abbott's hands. Perceiving "clearly" that "the initiative" had been taken by Captain Abbott, he might surely have offered Sirdar Chuttur Singh a full pardon, conditional on his proving the plea that he had resorted to none but defensive measures, and had acted only "for the protection of himself and the troops", when they were hemmed in by the insurgent mountaineers.

* *Papers, Punjaub*, 1849, p. 289.
† *Ibid.*, p. 291.
‡ *Ibid.*, p. 311.
§ *Ibid.*, p. 306.

No such offer was made to Chuttur Singh. No such offer was proposed or sanctioned by the Resident. No one told the Sikh Governor that the Resident had by no means decided hastily, like Captain Abbott, that Canora had been foully murdered. No hint was given that any question or dispute between him and Captain Abbott could possibly be open to investigation. No promise was made to Chuttur Singh but that of his life; no terms were offered him but those of implicit submission to Captain Abbott, against whose aggression he complained, and with these terms was coupled the intimation that he was dismissed from his Government, and that his landed property would be confiscated!

Captain Nicholson declared that Sirdar Chuttur Singh's conduct was the result of "terror and anxiety",* and he never deviated from that opinion. He told the Resident that the demand for the men who killed the unfortunate Commandant of Artillery would prove "an insurmountable obstacle", and that Chuttur Singh would "never accede to any terms" but "a free pardon." Yet on receiving overtures from Chuttur Singh, he "insisted, as a preliminary, on the Artillery Commandant's murderers being given up."† And on the 20th August he wrote to the Resident as follows :—

> "Considering how extremely desirable it is that matters should, if possible, be peaceably arranged, believing, also, that the Sirdar's conduct of late, though heinous in many respects, *had its origin in fear,* I have taken upon myself the responsibility of offering him the following terms, which, whether he accept (as Jhunda Singh seems to think he will) or not, I hope will meet your approval, *viz.*—That if the Sirdar immediately come into me, and send back the troops to their posts, I guarantee his life and izzut" (honour) "being spared; *but I neither guarantee his Nazimship nor his Jagheer, which, indeed, I have intimated to him he cannot expect to be allowed to retain.*
>
> "All things considered, I trust you will agree with me, that the loss of the Nizamut and of his Jagheer will be a sufficient punishment, and that I have acted rightly in offering these terms."‡

This severe sentence, without trial and without judgment, was instantly, by return of post, "entirely approved,

* *Papers, Punjaub*, 1849, p. 308.
† *Ibid.*, p. 284.
‡ *Ibid.*, p. 295.

confirmed and ratified" by the Resident, in a letter dated the 23rd August, to Captain Nicholson.*

Yet on the very day, the 23rd August, on which the Resident "confirmed and ratified" the degradation of Chuttur Singh and the resumption of his estates, he wrote as follows to Major Edwardes :—" Lieutenant Nicholson and Major Lawrence, with the best opportunities of judging, entirely concur with me that the Sirdar's conduct is owing more to his distrust and fear of Captain Abbott's feelings and intentions towards himself and the troops, than to any other cause."† He had previously remarked, in a letter to the Commander-in-Chief :—" Lieutenant Nicholson *does not seem to know the manner of Commandant Canora's death ; he calls it a murder*, and says that he understands Sirdar Chuttur Singh headed the party that killed him."‡ And on the 24th August, the day after he had approved and confirmed the hard terms proposed by Captain Nicholson, the Resident wrote to Captain Abbott, disapproving of much of his conduct, pronouncing it to have been "far from judicious", and that he was not justified "in calling the death of Commedan Canora a murder."§

On the 5th September the Resident writes to Government :—"I have promised him" (Chuttur Singh) "merely life, and an honourable investigation into his conduct."‖ How could that be "an honourable investigation", which was preceded by the infliction of heavy penalties ? The Sirdar was not even told that, if he succeeded in clearing himself, these penalties would be remitted.

When Chuttur Singh found that his appeal to the President and the Durbar was fruitless ; that Captain Abbott's proceedings were not disavowed, or, to his knowledge, disapproved ; and that no terms were offered to him but bare life, what could he think but that he had been marked down as the first victim in the general ruin of the Punjaub State ? Already alarmed and disgusted by the Maharanee's removal and ill-treatment, and by the evasive answer as to the Maharajah's marriage, his head may probably have been full of plots and projects,

* *Papers, Punjaub*, 1849, p. 297.
† *Ibid.*, p. 297.
‡ *Ibid.*, p. 286.
§ *Ibid.*, p. 316.
‖ *Ibid.*, p. 329.

and he may have been intently watching the course of events, when Captain Abbott's initiative threw him into an equivocal position. When that officer was permitted to pursue what he himself called "the work of destruction", unreproved, so far as Chuttur Singh knew, —when the plan of setting up Mahomedans against Sikhs, and reviving ancient blood feuds, was adopted and sanctioned by the highest British authorities, the old Sirdar's disaffection was confirmed. He was driven to desperation; he no longer resisted the importunities of the fanatic Sikhs among his followers and the troops. He plunged into open rebellion, and devoted himself to one last struggle for his religion and the Khalsa Raj.

And from the manner in which Chuttur Singh with the Sikh troops, and Captain Abbott with his Mahomedan peasants, were left by the Resident to fight it out by themselves, the Sikhs at other stations were soon persuaded that such was the settled plan of the British Government. Major George Lawrence* writes from Peshawur on the 5th of September:—"Colonel Ootar Singh declared that men from different Regiments had called on all to march on my quarters, as it was my intention to destroy all the Sikhs, *by raising the Mahomedan population.*

When Sirdar Chuttur Singh was fully committed beyond all possibility of retreat or redemption,—when redress was refused, and he was sentenced without judgment,—his sons threw in their lot with their father, and the second Sikh war began. Until they took that step, the Mooltan rebellion was isolated,—confined, indeed, within the walls of the fortress; although its importance was enhanced and the dangers attending it were aggravated by the Maharanee's removal, by our military vacillation and delay, and by the rumours of impending annexation. Up to the middle of September 1848, no Chief of note or distinction had joined in the insurrection. Captain Abbott's notion of a general conspiracy throughout the Punjaub, in which all the members of the Durbar and Maharajah Golab Singh of Cashmere were

* Now General Sir George St. Patrick Lawrence, elder brother of the late Lord Lawrence.

implicated, as well as his charge against Chuttur Singh of having been accessory before the fact to the Mooltan outbreak, are conclusively disproved by the dates and incidents of each successive convulsion. "As yet", writes the Resident on the 8th September, "no Chief has, openly, joined Sirdar Chuttur Singh." "Neither the army beyond Hazara, nor the Chiefs generally, appear to have been prepared for this move of Sirdar Chuttur Singh."

"If Rajah Shere Singh should not join his father, supposing the rebellion to gain head, it will be very surprising; and it is equally surprising that the Sirdar should have taken his decided line, without having secured the concurrence of his son."*

Two facts, in particular, show that Chuttur Singh had not secured the concurrence of his son, and that neither of them had any complicity with Dewan Moolraj of Mooltan,—first, the good conduct of Rajah Shere Singh until the middle of September, and, secondly, the surprise and mistrust of the Dewan Moolraj at Shere Singh's tardy defection.

Major Edwardes believes that Rajah Shere Singh undertook his share in the task of suppressing the rebellion of Dewan Moolraj with the best intentions.† So determined did Rajah Shere Singh appear, up to the end of August 1848, to check the disloyalty of his men, that he was reviled as a Mussulman,—the greatest reproach that can be cast upon a Sikh,‡—and a conspiracy was detected to put him to death by poison. When this crime was fully brought home to the ringleader, Shoojan Singh, "a Sikh jagheerdar horseman of some consideration and still greater notoriety", the Rajah "carried the extreme sentence of the law into effect, and caused the traitor to be blown from one of his own guns", in his own camp. "The act," Major Edwardes adds, "was extremely unpopular in the Rajah's force, and I rather think that he himself expected resistance."§

Reviewing all these transactions two years later, Major

* *Punjaub Papers*, 1849, p. 333.

† *Ibid.*, p. 244; *A Year on the Punjaub Frontier*, vol. ii, pp. 420, 425.

‡ *Papers, Punjaub*, 1849, pp. 330, 344.

§ *Ibid.*, pp. 329, 330.

Edwardes says:—"The question with which I am concerned in this event is, 'When did Shere Singh resolve to join his father?' I have no hesitation whatever in stating that it is now as certain as anything in this world can be, that it was on the 12th or 13th of September,—certainly within forty-eight hours of the fatal step being taken."*

Moolraj was quite unprepared for the desertion of Rajah Shere Singh. He had done his best to corrupt the Sikh soldiers in Shere Singh's camp, but the Rajah himself had rejected all his overtures. The consequence was that "Moolraj could not believe that Shere Singh had come over in good faith",—"withdrew all his own soldiers within the walls of Mooltan", and made the Rajah's army "take their places in the British front", under the walls of the Fort.† In a few days Shere Singh was disgusted with Moolraj's suspicions, and went off to join his father.

The Resident writes to Government on the 23rd of September:—"Rajah Shere Singh's conduct has been very extraordinary, and is almost inexplicable."‡ It was indeed inexplicable, except upon the very obvious presumption that he had decided to make an effort, at all hazards, for the assistance of his injured father, and for the existence of the Sikh sovereignty, which he began to see was doomed. Still, but for his father's wrongs, he would rather have trusted to the good faith and generosity of what he knew to be the stronger side. On or about the 10th of September, Shere Singh received letters from his father,§ in which the old Chief, without doubt, informed him of the heavy penalties to which he had been sentenced; and on the 14th, in a "fit of desperation and confusion",‖ the son consented to espouse the cause of his father, and to make it the cause of the nation. And in the private and secret letter to his brother, Golab Singh, at Lahore, Rajah Shere Singh expressly declares that he has taken this step in consequence of Captain Abbott's conduct to his father. "The Singh Sahib" (Sirdar

* *A Year on the Punjaub Frontier*, vol. ii, p. 503.

† *Ibid.*, p. 515.

‡ *Papers, Punjaub*, 1849, p. 360.

§ *Ibid.*, p. 343.

‖ *Ibid.*, 358.

Chuttur Singh) "has several times written to me, stating that he constantly obeyed Captain Abbott's directions, but that officer, acting according to the suggestions of the people of Hazara", (the Mahomedans) "has treated him most unjustly, and caused him much grief and trouble; and that he has also exerted himself to destroy and disperse the Khalsa troops." He adds, "I resolved, therefore, yesterday, to join the Singh Sahib, and devote myself to the cause of our religion".* All idea, therefore, of a deep conspiracy on the part of either Rajah Shere Singh or Sirdar Chuttur Singh, is completely negatived. Chuttur Singh was goaded into hostilities by Captain Abbott's aggression, and his son was driven to join him in what they both felt to be a desperate rebellion, by the refusal of redress, and the multiplied rumours and symptoms of the Raj having been doomed to destruction.

But everything tends to prove that the original outbreak at Mooltan was equally unpremeditated. The Dewan Moolraj was rich, in infirm health and without children, timid, unpopular with the army and people; and the Resident reports that immediately before the catastrophe he had "only five or six field guns",† and "had discharged almost all his regular troops, preparatory to resigning his government".‡ The attack on the two British officers sent to relieve him of his post, was caused by a sudden impulse of discontent and fanaticism, in the results of which, after a vain attempt to quell it, Moolraj felt himself irretrievably compromised. With hope of scant mercy from the British Government, and certain of death from the mutinous soldiery, if he trusted to that mercy, he yielded to circumstances, and accepted the lot that fate flung before him.§

Before the murderous outbreak at Mooltan, the Dewan, as we have just remarked, had discharged almost all his regular troops. That had been the order of the day for

* *Papers, Punjaub*, p. 359; *A Year on the Punjaub Frontier*, vol. ii, p. 505.

† *Papers, Punjaub*, 1849, p. 133. Lord Dalhousie's final opinion is that "the first outbreak was unpremeditated, and, in a manner, accidental".—*Papers, Punjaub*, 1849, p. 585.

‡ *Ibid.*, p. 371.

§ *Ibid.*, p. 151; *A Year on the Punjaub Frontier*, vol. ii, p. 165.

more than a year all over the Punjaub. Between 10,000 and 20,000 soldiers had been disbanded before April 1847 ;* and towards the close of that month the Resident speaks of gradually reducing the Infantry "from 20,000 to 15,000 men, and the Sowars" (Cavalry) "from 12,000 to 10,000".† The reports from every province describe the same process of reduction. Mr. Agnew, who was sent in company with a Sikh Governor to take over charge from Dewan Moolraj, is instructed to give his "early attention" to "reducing all unnecessary Irregulars"; the best men from the Regular Regiments serving at Mooltan are to be picked out and sent to Lahore ; "the remaining men may be paid up and discharged".‡ Thus the military class at Mooltan,—not, be it observed, conscripts, but soldiers by hereditary profession,—not only knew what was in store for them under the new administration, but actually had a foretaste of it before the British officers arrived. Moolraj, not well pleased with his forced retirement, must have felt a malicious satisfaction, when dismissing his troops, in explaining to them the cause of that unpopular measure. We cannot, therefore, be surprised to learn that the man who led the attack on the British officers as they passed over the drawbridge of Mooltan, was a soldier, "brooding, perchance", as Major Edwardes wrote, "over his own long services and probable dismissal",§ nor that the subsequent acts, by which Moolraj was effectually involved in rebellion, and "the crowning crime of assassination", were perpetrated by the Sikh troops.||

For some years before the Sutlej campaign, all the power of the Punjaub State had been wielded by the Sikh soldiery, through their Punchayuts, or elected committees. They had raised and deposed a succession of Princes and ministers ; in every political conjuncture their favour had to be propitiated by largesses and augmented pay. The Sikh army claimed the privilege of representing, as a corporate body, the Khalsa,—the elect and holy race of true believers. Lord Hardinge, writing to the Court of Directors on the 30th September 1845,

* *Papers, Punjaub*, 1849, p. 2. † *Ibid.*, p. 6. ‡ *Ibid.*, p. 126.
§ *A Year on the Punjaub Frontier*, vol. ii, p. 51. || *Ibid.*, p. 161.

says that "the most influential and leading Chiefs" feel "their personal interests" to be "endangered by the democratic revolution so successfully accomplished by the Sikh army".* Even the Maharanee saw her own brother, Jowahir Singh, shot down before her own eyes, by the sentence of this armed Inquisition.

In the Duke of Argyll's own words:—"It was the Khalsa army, not the Lahore Government, which began the Sikh war. The great force which Runjeet had brought together, and had disciplined with admirable efficiency for the purposes of war, was an army whose fierce fanaticism, inflamed by concentration and by the sense of power, had become incapable of control."†

The victories of Lord Gough, and the occupation of Lahore, put an end to the Prætorian Parliament. The Punchayuts were no longer recognised or allowed to assemble. Discipline was restored and enforced. Military license was restrained. The political influence of the army was annihilated.

The Sirdars, who for years had trembled under the thraldom of the Sikh Punchayuts, rejoiced at their subjugation. But the unruly fanatics who had organised and guided those short-lived democratic institutions, were, of course, furious at their downfall, and, though somewhat dejected and discouraged by the recent crushing disaster, only waited for an opportunity to claim their representative functions, and to regain their former ascendency.

In every scene throughout the insurrectionary crisis the same incidents repeat themselves. The Sikh soldiers try to force on a rebellion, opposed and resisted by the nobles and landholders, and even by their regimental officers. It was so, even by Captain Abbott's account, with the Sikh Brigade which he suspected and surrounded in Hazara. "The officers," he writes, "received his" (Chuttur Singh's) "orders with distrust, demurred, delayed, but were finally borne along by the men."‡ According to him, Sirdar Chuttur Singh "ordered them" (the troops) "to destroy an innocent and loyal man, and

* *Papers respecting the late Hostilities, etc.*, 1846, p. 6.

† *India under Dalhousie and Canning*, p. 55.

‡ *Papers, Punjaub*, 1849, p. 303.

to mutiny against my authority, *and that of their officers*."*

Captain Nicholson writes to the Resident:—"If the Sikh troops in Hazara were under the control of their officers, there would be no difficulty; but, as usual in the Sikh army, few or none of the officers have any influence with the men."†

Major George Lawrence writes from Peshawur:—"I really believe that most of the officers are very desirous to keep their troops to their allegiance."

The Resident, shortly after the bad news from Mooltan writes:—"The Sikh *Sirdars* whom I have sent may be implicitly relied upon, and the influence which they have with the soldiery they will make the best use of. But the soldiery themselves are not equally trustworthy; they are dispirited; not satisfied with their Sirdars; and have, as may be supposed, no very kindly feeling for us."§ On the 22nd of June, he wrote again:—"*The Sirdars* are true, I believe; the soldiers are all false, I know."‖

On the 13th of July, Major Edwardes reported thus to the Resident:—"With respect to *the Sirdars*, I believe them to be heart and soul on our side, which is the side of jaghires, titles, employments, and whole throats. But their force, with equal confidence, I report to be against us to a man."¶

The Resident writes to Government on the 17th June 1848:—

"On the night of the 8th instant, the Churunjeet Regiment of Cavalry broke into open mutiny: *the Sirdars* succeeded, with some difficulty, in preventing the Artillery and the Infantry Regiment from joining them."**

Many of the Sirdars were by degrees drawn into the tide, particularly after the Maharanee's exile, and the defection of Chuttur Singh and his sons, but they went reluctantly and doubtfully, and in some cases were evidently dragged into it by the troops. The Sirdars, in fact, had something to lose. The Sikh soldiers had lost

* *Papers, Punjaub*, 1849, p. 311.
† *Ibid.*, p. 307.
‡ *Ibid.*, p. 340.
§ *Ibid.*, p. 137.
‖ *Ibid.*, p. 220.
¶ *Ibid.*, p. 254.
** *Ibid.*, p. 217.

nearly everything; and they saw that if a reformed system were firmly established in the Punjaub, their occupation was gone. As the British administration was more completely introduced, they found their organisation broken up, their special privileges abolished, their pay lowered,* and their numbers reduced. Of course they were ripe for revolt.

The Resident, Sir Frederick Currie, writes as follows on the 27th of September 1848 :—"The Sikh soldiers of the old régime can never again be trusted; and I must say that, to my knowledge, *Rajah Tej Singh said, two years ago, and has always adhered to the opinion, that it was less dangerous, and would prove less embarrassing, to disband them all, and raise a new army, than to continue a man of them in service.*"†

We did not take Rajah Tej Singh's advice; but, on the contrary, as the Resident said, kept up the old Sikh troops, as "the disciplined army of the country, and left in their hands all the artillery and munitions of war."‡

Chronic mutiny had existed in the Sikh army for six years, sustained by religious fanaticism, and swelled by continued success to the dimensions of a democratic revolution. We knew it; we were warned of it. Nothing occurred in 1848 that was not contemplated and expressly provided for, when the British Government undertook, in December 1846, the office of Guardian during the minority of Maharajah Duleep Singh. The several extensions of the British protective occupation were conceded by Lord Hardinge, at the urgent request of the Durbar, with special reference to "the reorganisation of the army".§ That was recognised on all sides, throughout the negotiations, as the great requirement and the great peril. Lord Hardinge, writing to the Resident on the 7th of December 1846, declares that he "cannot permit the renewal of a state of anarchy and *military despotism*, similar to that which existed last year".|| Within ten days of this despatch

* *Papers respecting the late Hostilities, etc.*, 1846, pp. 95, 96.

† *Papers, Punjaub*, 1849, p. 377. ‡ *Ibid.*, p. 217.

§ *Further Papers respecting the late Hostilities, etc.*, 1846, pp. 95, 103. *Papers, Articles of Agreement, etc.*, 1847, p. 5.

|| *Papers, Articles of Agreement*, 1847, p. 42.

being written, the Articles of Agreement were signed at Lahore, on the 16th December 1846, embodying the only terms on which the Governor-General would consent to the continuance of a British force at Lahore, and by which "unlimited authority in all matters, during the Maharajah's minority", were conferred upon the British Resident.*

"The immediate effect," says Lord Hardinge, "of depriving a numerous body of military adventurers of employment (there being still many to be disbanded to reduce the numbers to the limits of the Treaty of Lahore), may be troublesome, and a source of some uneasiness. No policy can at once get rid of an evil which has been the growth of years."†

"I see around me", writes the Resident, Sir Henry Lawrence, in April 1847, "and hear of, so many men, who, having been Generals and Colonels in the Sikh army, are now struggling for existence; and, at the same time, know that so little justice has been done even in recent reductions, that my great wonder has been the good conduct of the Sikh army during the last twelvemonth."

"I am well aware that neither independent feelings, nor lawless habits, are easily eradicated: and I am quite satisfied that there is nothing too foolish, nothing too desperate, for Asiatic zealots or desperadoes to attempt. I endeavour therefore to be on the alert."‡

In June 1847, he writes as follows:—"It is wise to keep before our eyes the fact that the animus of unrest and insurrection slumbers, but is not yet dead, in the Punjaub. It would be a miracle if it were otherwise; for assuredly the habits acquired during six years of anarchy are not to be laid aside in a month or a year.§

It is clear, then, that neither Lord Hardinge, nor Sir Henry Lawrence, the Resident whom he appointed, expected to be immediately free from all danger of military mutiny or rebellion. The following extract is taken from the *History of India*, by Mr. J. C. Marshman.

* *Papers, Articles of Agreement*, 1847, p. 24.
† *Ibid.*, p. 25.
‡ *Papers, Punjaub*, 1849, pp. 6, 7. § *Ibid.*

"The precautionary measures adopted by Lord Hardinge manifested equal foresight and vigour. He did not expect that a country teeming with disbanded soldiers, the bravest and most haughty in India, who had been nurtured in victory and conquest, and pampered with seven years of military licence, would be as free from disturbance as a district in Bengal. To provide for the prompt suppression of any insurrectionary movements which might arise, he organised three moveable Brigades, complete in carriage and equipment, each of which consisted of one European corps, three Regiments of Native Infantry and one of Cavalry, with twelve guns, chiefly of European Horse Artillery. These were held in readiness at Lahore, Jullunder and Ferozepore, to take the field at the shortest notice."*

Yet on the very first occasion of the peace of the country being disturbed, the Resident, Sir Frederick Currie, writes to Lord Dalhousie :—"Dewan Moolraj is an officer of the Sikh Government; he is in rebellion, if in rebellion at all, to the Sikh Durbar, and the orders of that Government. The coercion must come from the Sikh Government, *unaided by British troops, if possible. If it should be necessary to move a British soldier, the affair will be a serious one for the Durbar.*"†

"I could not consent, under any circumstances, to send a British force on such an expedition, *whatever may be the result and consequence of the state of things which will follow, to the continuance of the Sikh Government.*‡

And this, although the British troops were there, under treaty, and were subsidised, for that very service of maintaining the Sikh Government, and preserving "the peace of the country."§

"The principal Sirdars started this morning, under the impression that the British column would follow. I have sent for them back, to explain to them that they must, by their own resources, put down the rebellion of their own Governor, aided by their own troops and their officers, and bring the perpetrators to punishment."||

So soon was the menacing note of annexation sounded in the ears of the Sikh Sirdars. And this language,

* Marshman's *History of India*, 1867, vol. iii, p. 305.
† *Papers, Punjaub*, 1849, p. 133. ‡ *Ibid.*, p. 139.
§ *Papers, Articles of Agreement*, 1847, pp. 49, 50, 51.
|| *Papers, Punjaub*, p. 140.

natural and excusable in the first excitement, indignation, and perplexity of a sudden and alarming crisis, pervades, with some intermittence and inconsistency, all the Resident's correspondence, and is at last deliberately adopted by the Governor-General in pronouncing his final judgment.

On the 27th April, the Resident continues his narrative.

> "The Chiefs returned yesterday morning, and having heard what I had to say regarding the necessity of their putting down the rebellion, and bringing the offenders to justice, by their own means, *as the only hope of saving their Government*, they retired to consult and concert measures.
>
> "After much discussion they declared themselves unable, without British aid, to coerce Dewan Moolraj in Mooltan, and bring the perpetrators of the outrage to justice. They admitted that their troops were not to be depended on to act against Moolraj, especially the regular army of the State, and they recommended that these corps should be kept in their former positions, to maintain the peace, and prevent, as far as possible, the spread of the rebellion. This service they thought the Sikh troops might be depended on to perform, under the arrangements they proposed for the Chiefs, with their personal followers, going out themselves into the Provinces,—more especially if speedy measures were taken by the British Government for the occupation of Mooltan."*

There can be no question that this advice was the best possible for the time. If it had been taken, the rebellion would have been speedily crushed. It was not taken. This discussion took place on April 26th, 1848. But it was not until August 18th, after an interval of four months, that the British troops, under General Whish, arrived before Mooltan.† The siege was raised on September 14th, in consequence of the defection of Rajah Shere Singh.‡ It was not until December 26th, 1848, that the Force under General Whish, having been strengthened by a Division from Bombay, resumed its old position before Mooltan, after three months and a half more of inaction, during which period the Commander-in-Chief had made no military movement to arrest Chuttur Singh's operations, or to support the British officers in

* *Papers, Punjaub*, 1849, p. 140.
† *Ibid.*, p. 291.
‡ *Ibid.*, p. 355.

the more distant posts. Mooltan was taken in a week after the renewal of the siege; the Dewan Moolraj surrended himself unconditionally on January 22nd, 1849. But, in the meanwhile, the mischief was done; these long delays, these retrogressive and suspensive manœuvres, had given double force to all other provocations and temptations. The Punjaub was in a blaze. Rajah Shere Singh was now at the head of 30,000 men, with 60 guns. The drawn battle of Chillianwalla was fought on January 13th, 1849. On February 21st, Lord Gough, reinforced by the whole of General Whish's army, gained the crowning victory of Goojerat; and on March 14th, Sirdar Chuttur Singh, Rajah Shere Singh, and other Chiefs gave up their swords; and the remains of the Sikh army, to the number of 16,000 men, laid down their arms. So ended the second Punjaub war,—eleven months having elapsed since the first outbreak at Mooltan. Not a British soldier was moved for the first three months. After the first failure to take Mooltan, there was a total cessation of active efforts in the field for three months more, from the middle of September to the middle of December 1848.

Every one had foreseen the inevitable effect of these dilatory measures. Throughout the Blue Book are scattered innumerable expressions of opinion by the Resident and his Assistants, that any long delay in punishing the mutinous outrage at Mooltan, would act as an irresistible encouragement to military ambition, and an incitement to Sikh fanaticism. Major Edwardes says:—"It was my own belief at the time, that had the Mooltan rebellion been put down at once, the Sikh insurrection would never have grown out of it; it was a belief shared, moreover, (as well as I remember,) by every political officer in the Punjaub, and I for one still think so now."*

On June 22nd, 1848, Major Edwardes, having with the troops of the Nawab of Bhawulpoor, a force of 18,000 men and 30 guns under his command, all well-disposed, and in high spirits at their two recent victories, proposed to the Resident to commence the seige of Mooltan forthwith, asking only for a few heavy guns, and an Engineer

* *A Year on the Punjaub Frontier*, vol. ii, p. 145.

officer with a detachment of Sappers.* And two years later he writes :—

"In June and up to the end of July, I am quite sure that Lieutenant Lake's force and my own could have taken the city of Mooltan with the utmost facility; for it was surrounded by nothing stronger than a venerable brick wall, and the rebel army was dispirited by its losses at Kineyree and Suddoosam. On this point neither Lieutenant Lake nor myself, nor General Cortlandt (who was an older, and therefore a steadier soldier than either of us) had ever any doubt."†

Major Robert Napier of the Engineers,‡ writing from Mooltan on September 14th, just as General Whish was compelled to raise the siege, explains the effect of the long delay on the *personnel* of the rebel army. "Moolraj's forces are now very different from what they were when Edwardes met them. Except a few, the Irregulars have been exchanged for the old Sikh soldiers."§

But the veteran Chief of the Indian army could not "consent to an insufficient force, such as one Brigade of any strength, being sent", and preferred to wait "until the proper season for military operations" (the cold season) "should arrive."‖

If these dilatory measures were adopted in perfect good faith,—and I have no doubt that they were by the military authorities,—I should not hesitate to condemn them as unstatesmanlike and blundering.

If they were not adopted in perfect good faith,—"if", as has often been hinted, "the delay in crushing the rebellion sprang in part from a secret hope of its spreading far enough to furnish Government with a fair excuse for annexing the whole dominions of Runjeet Singh",¶—such a policy can only be characterised as unprincipled and unjustifiable.

But whether the dilatory plan was unstatesmanlike or unprincipled,—whether it was a blunder or a trick,—nay, even if it was the wisest possible, and in every respect

* *Papers, Punjaub*, 1849, p. 223.

† *A Year on the Punjaub Frontier*, vol. ii, p. 403.

‡ Now Lord Napier of Magdala, G.C.B., etc.

§ *Papers, Punjaub*, 1849, p. 356. ‖ *Ibid.*, pp. 238, 239.

¶ Trotter's *History of India from* 1844 *to* 1862 (Allen, 1866), vol. i, p. 134.

justifiable,—my position is unaffected. It was emphatically *our* work. It was a plan deliberately adopted by the Resident and the Governor-General, contrary to the advice of the Council of Regency. It was the plan of Lord Dalhousie, administering, "with unlimited powers", under treaty, the government of the Punjaub. It was the plan of the Guardian, managing the affairs of his Ward.

Lord Dalhousie's procedure in settling the future relations of the Punjaub with British India after the campaign of 1849, just amounts to this:—a Guardian, having undertaken, for a valuable consideration, a troublesome and dangerous trust, declares, on the first occurrence of those troubles and dangers, of which he had full knowledge and fore-warning, that, as a compensation for his exertions and a protection for the future, he shall appropriate his Ward's estate and personal property to his own purposes. And this, although the Guardian holds ample security in his own hands for the repayment of any outlay, and the satisfaction of any damages he might have incurred, in executing the conditions of the trust.

We have quoted the Resident's refusal to send a British force to Mooltan, "whatever may be the consequences of the state of things which will follow to the continuance of the Sikh Government." In the same dispatch he writes to Lord Dalhousie as follows:—

> "Your Lordship will, I fear, have to consider how far it is incumbent upon us, how far it is possible for us, to maintain an engagement with a Government, which, in the persons of its Chiefs, its soldiers, and its people, repays our endeavours for its maintenance by perfidy and outrage, and is powerless to afford us redress.
>
> "Doubtless we have reduced it to its state of weakness, but we are not responsible for its treachery and violation of trust."*

At this time no "Chiefs", except the Dewan Moolraj of Mooltan, had committed any offence; no "soldiers", except those at Mooltan, had taken part in any perfidy or outrage; and the "people" had not moved in the matter at all.

Dewan Moolraj was not a Sikh: he and his father had

* *Papers, Punjaub*, 18:9, p. 140.

governed Mooltan for thirty years, with almost independent sway; they had fortified the city with the scarcely disguised object of holding their own against the Sikh Government, whose power they had repeatedly defied,—once during the British occupation of Lahore, before the transfer of authority to the Resident.* If Moolraj, therefore, rebelled again, it was nothing to be surprised at,—nothing but what ought to have been, and must have been, contemplated and prepared for, when we assumed the administration of the Punjaub. Yet the Resident speaks of this occurrence as something prodigious and unheard of; and denounces the Sikh Government,—over which he was presiding, with unlimited powers,—as guilty of "perfidy and outrage, in the persons" of the refractory vassal and turbulent soldiery, whom the Durbar, by imploring British assistance, had confessed themselves unable to coerce.

This inability, also, is made a charge against the Durbar by the Resident, and a pretext for no longer maintaining our engagement with it; although its inability to control the Chiefs and the army, was the main cause of that engagement being made. It is "powerless", he complains, "to afford us redress." He adds:—"Doubtless we have reduced it to its state of weakness." The Government of the Punjaub was *not* powerless; but all its power was concentrated in the hands of the British Resident. Its power mainly consisted in the British troops, subsidised from the revenues of the country, which the Resident hesitated to employ. Without the aid of the British troops, to which it was entitled by treaty, it was, of course, in "a state of weakness", and to that state of weakness, as the Resident admits, we had depressed it. The visible British occupation and notorious transfer of power to the Resident, tended to destroy the personal influence of the Sirdars, while the substitution of a British force for the disbanded Sikh troops, placed the means of executive supremacy beyond their reach. Both the physical and moral force at the disposal of the Durbar, apart from the Resident's support, was greatly diminished.

* *Papers, Punjaub*, 1849, pp. 5, 117.

The scheme for the reduction and reorganisation of the army seems to have been most judicious,—though, perhaps, the more sweeping measure proposed by Rajah Tej Singh, would have been safer and more effectual,—and it appears to have been carried out with great consideration, and with many countervailing advantages for the humbler and less ambitious soldiers, especially for those who were not Sikhs. But it was a most critical and delicate operation, and it was emphatically *our* work.

By the unlimited authority entrusted to the Resident, the numerical strength of the Sikh army had been lowered, until every town and village was filled with the discontented brethren of those who were still retained in the ranks, whose disaffection was at the same time enhanced by a stricter discipline, curtailed privileges, and the downfall of their political and religious preponderance.

It could not be expected,—we have seen that it was not expected by Lord Hardinge and Sir Henry Lawrence,—that this transition stage would be passed through in perfect tranquillity. Yet the Resident declaims against "the perfidy and outrage",—"treachery and violation of trust",—"spoliation and crime",*—committed at Mooltan, as unprecedented and unimaginable, and imputes it all to the Sikh Government, "in the persons" of the mutinous soldiery, who, during six years had domineered over all authority, who had murdered three Prime Ministers and several Princes, and whose subjection was the special task we had engaged to perform.

We knew what we were about when we assumed the Guardianship of a Prince whose dominions had suffered from six years of anarchy. We undertook the obligations of suppressing military mutiny and civil war,—"of preserving the peace of the country", with British troops subsidised for the purpose. Furthermore, we obtained by the Treaty unlimited military powers throughout the Punjaub,—the right of holding all the strong places and positions, the right of disbanding and enlisting troops. It may have been hoped, but it can never

* *Papers, Punjaub*, 1849, p. 141.

have been expected, that everything would go on smoothly, that our troops would never be actively employed,—that none of those scenes of violence and bloodshed, which had compelled the Durbar to entreat our aid, would recur during the British occupation. For the term of our Guardianship,—the minority of Duleep Singh—we demanded full powers, we accepted full responsibility.

Lord Dalhousie admits his full responsibility, as the Guardian of British interests, for the inordinate military delays which swelled the Mooltan rebellion into a war, but does not seem to feel any responsibility at all, as the trustee and administrator of the Punjaub State, and the Guardian of its infant Maharajah. "On the one hand", he writes, "it was impossible to doubt that, if there existed in the minds of the people of the Punjaub any inclination to rise against the British power, a delay in visiting the outrage committed at Mooltan, and the apparent impunity of the offender, would give strong encouragement to an outbreak which might spread over the whole Punjaub. On the other hand, it was equally clear that there would be serious danger to the health and to the very existence of European troops", if they were to carry on "military operations in the hot and rainy months."*

It might have occurred to the Governor-General and the Commander-in-Chief that the loss of life among the European and Native troops of our army, and the general destruction of life and property in the Punjaub, would be much greater in the event of a general rebellion, than could possibly be caused by the march of one Brigade of British troops in the hot and rainy months. And as it might have been anticipated, so it proved. "Strange to say", writes Mr. J. C. Marshman, "it was found that General Whish's troops were more healthy during their progress to Mooltan than they had been in cantonments, and it was manifest that the unsuitableness of the season, which was urged as a ground of objection to an early and prompt movement, was a mere bugbear."†

* *Papers, Punjaub*, 1849, p. 656.

† *History of India*, vol. iii, p. 319.

These were Sir Henry Lawrence's reflections on the military plans of 1848 :—"We cannot afford in India to shilly-shally and talk of weather and seasons. If we are not ready to take the field at all seasons, we have no business here."*

On the whole, however, Lord Dalhousie concludes that "it can never now be determined whether the immediate commencement at that time" (the hot season) "of the siege of Mooltan would or would not have averted the war. But this, at least", he adds, "is certain, that if the short delay which took place in punishing the murder of two British officers at Mooltan"—a short delay of nine months !†—"could produce an universal rising against us throughout all the Punjaub, the very fact itself betokens the existence of a deep and widespread feeling of hostility against us, which could not long have been repressed".‡

We shall see that the "rising" was by no means "universal", and that Lord Dalhousie's denunciations of the Sirdars and the people of the Punjaub were highly exaggerated.

Lord Dalhousie continues his argument as follows :—"The worst that can be alleged, therefore, against the delay is, that it precipitated the crisis; and opened, somewhat earlier, to the Sikhs that opportunity for renewal of war, which, sooner or later, so bitter a spirit of hostility must have created for itself."

Major Edwardes agrees with Lord Dalhousie on this point; he, also, thinks the struggle was inevitable, sooner or later. He expresses his belief, in passages already quoted, that "had the Mooltan rebellion been put down, the Sikh insurrection would never have grown out of it", and that, with very moderate assistance from Lahore, he could have taken Mooltan in June. He indicates as plainly as is consistent with modesty, and a decent respect for seniors and official superiors, his opinion that the delay was, both in a military and political point of view,

* Kaye's *Indian Officers* (Allen, 1867), vol. ii, pp. 397, 298.

† Mr. Vans Agnew and Lieutenant Anderson were murdered on the 20th April 1848; the citadel of Mooltan was surrendered by the Dewan Moolraj on January 22nd, 1849.

‡ *Papers, Punjaub*, 1849, p. 657.

an error of judgment. But he says, in his table of Contents to the volume :—"The Author shows that it was providential." In the text he observes :—"Far from regarding this as a matter for regret, I see in it only the strongest example that ever came within my own experience, of human judgment overruled by Providence for good."*

The "good", according to Major Edwardes, was that "the whole of the Punjaub was annexed to British India in March 1849"; whereas, "if the most favourable circumstances had succeeded, and on the 4th of September 1854, the Governor-General, in fulfilment of Treaties permitted to remain in force", had withdrawn the British troops, and handed over the Punjaub to its youthful Sovereign, "with a revenue improved by peace, an exchequer replenished by honesty and economy, and an army improved by discipline", no one can believe "that the peace of the frontier would have lasted for a year, or a second Sikh war have been avoided".†

I cannot enter into the designs of Providence, but I freely acknowledge that Major Edwardes had many precedents for his assumption. Every conquest has been hailed as providential by the conqueror. "Te Deum" is sung by the victor for every victory.

Nor can a mere guess or surmise of what might have happened under different circumstances prove that a certain decision was wise, or just. If the annexation of the Punjaub was an iniquitous proceeding; if its iniquity has been made manifest, it is no reply to say either that it was Providential, or that it must have happened sooner or later.

This guess, or surmise, of the inveterate and inextinguishable hostility of the Sikhs, is, however, by no means warranted by the history of our previous relations with them, by the progress of events during the insurrection, or by our experience of other States and other races in India. No doubt there was a turbulent spirit abroad in 1848; there were elements of political and religious fanaticism pervading large classes in the Punjaub, espe-

* *A Year on the Punjaub Frontier*, vol. ii, p. 145.

† *Ibid.*, pp. 145, 146.

cially the Sikhs serving in the army, or connected with the soldiery. We knew all this when we undertook the Guardianship ; our protective occupation was invited expressly to meet those perils. No doubt this turbulent and fanatical spirit became hostile to the British occupation, and to the party of Sikh Sirdars who co-operated with the Resident, when the new administration was carrying into effect the reduction and restraint of the army. But there would have been the same hostility against a purely Native Government, if it had attempted to enforce, without British assistance, the same unpopular measures.

About the time of the bad news from Mooltan, however, everything indicated that the Punjaub was settling down into a state of peaceful industry. A general impression prevailed of the overwhelming and resistless power of the British Government, and of the moderation and justice of its policy. On April 6th, 1848, the Resident thus reported to the Governor-General :—

"Perfect tranquillity prevails, at present, throughout all the territories under the Lahore Government; and I have no reason to think that the apparent contentment of the people is other than real."

It is impossible to say exactly what permanent effect would have been produced on the habits and pursuits of the people, if tranquillity could have been preserved during the five years and a half of the Maharajah's minority that remained, according to the Treaty—if Lord Dalhousie had not decided in favour of annexation—when the insurrection was finally quelled in March 1849. If a judicious system had been brought into play, five or six years might have accustomed the people to the advantages of peace and order, and a strong Native Government might have been installed at Lahore.

Great changes for the better had certainly begun to tell in the first fifteen months of British occupation. A great advance had been made towards a state of political quietude, the best evidence of which is to be found in the slowness and reluctance with which the successive steps in the insurrection were taken.

Notwithstanding the dangerous excitement that undoubtedly prevailed throughout the lower ranks of the Sikh soldiery, both those in the service and those recently disbanded, there had been no extensive mutiny, or desertion of numerical importance, until Rajah Shere Singh went over to the enemy in September, from motives which we have already discussed. When Sirdar Chuttur Singh and his son, with the troops under their command, were openly co-operating with the Dewan Moolraj, who had now defied the British power for five months with impunity, when General Whish was obliged, as the result of Rajah Shere Singh's defection, to raise the siege of Mooltan, and wait for reinforcements,* a great stimulus was given to the ambition and fanaticism of the disaffected Sikhs throughout the Punjaub. And yet up to October 4th, the Resident writes, no Sirdar had joined Chuttur Singh,†, who had failed utterly to induce any of the Regular troops, except those who had been with him in Hazara, and against whom Captain Abbott had taken the initiative, to join his banner. He had marched "towards the camp of his son, Rajah Shere Singh and the other insurgents, in despair at the refusals he had received *from the Sikh officers at* Peshawur".‡ It was not until October that the troops at Bunnoo and Peshawur broke into mutiny,§ when Moolraj had held out for six months, and Chuttur Singh was, to all appearance, unchecked and unopposed.

Thus the main cause of an "unpremeditated and accidental"‖ outbreak, according to Lord Dalhousie, growing into a formidable insurrection, was the long delay before any attempt was made to punish the Dewan Moolraj,—a delay which, by degrees, raised him from a very low grade in popular estimation to the rank of the great heroes of Hindoo lore, and dissipated almost all the advantages of the brilliant success of Major Edwardes and General Cortlandt, at the head of the Maharajah's troops. This delay, astonishing and inexplicable to the people at large, was explained by the Resident to the most influential men of the country in a sense the most alarming and

* *Punjaub Papers*, 1849, p. 355.

† *Ibid.*, p. 381.

‡ *Ibid.*, pp. 390, 391.

§ *Ibid.*, pp. 375, 397.

‖ *Ante*, p. 40 (note).

exasperating possible. They were told that "they must put down the rebellion by their own resources, *as the only hope of saving their Government*". No wonder a rumour soon got abroad among the Sirdars and soldiery, as Major Edwardes tells us that "the British meditated declaring the Punjaub forfeited by the recent troubles and misconduct of the troops". The rumour was true.

As if to add more fuel to these inflammatory rumours, to stir up against us every feeling of loyalty and chivalry at the most critical moment, the Maharanee, "the mother of all the Sikhs", was suddenly deported from the country, and imprisoned at Benares, under circumstances which, we may be sure, assumed in the telling an aspect of violence and indignity. The effect upon the Sikh troops of this most ill-judged measure, was, as we have seen, immediate. The Ranee's influence was almost annihilated, when we made her a martyr, and it revived at once.

The rumour as to the impending annexation, the doubts as to his daughter's marriage with the Maharajah, and the facts as to the Ranee's persecution, may have already converted old Chuttur Singh into a conspirator, but it was the Mussulman insurrection of his own Province, instigated and headed by his colleague, Captain Abbott, unchecked and unreproved by the Resident, that compelled him to become a rebel.

Surely it is sufficiently obvious that among a warlike race and sect like the Sikhs,—so lately dominant throughout the Punjaub in Church and State,—and after the stirring events of the previous six years, these successive temptations and provocations could not but prove irresistible, and that they form an ample explanation of the phenomena and development of the second Punjaub war, without resorting to the unwarrantable surmise that "a renewal of war" was inevitable, and that our dilatory proceedings merely "precipitated the crisis". There is nothing to show that, without these delays and errors of judgment on our part, there would ever have been a crisis at all. But for the extraordinary temptations of our long inaction and apparent inability to cope with the rebellion,—but for the excitement caused by the well-founded rumours as to our bad intentions towards the Raj,—but for the provocations afforded by the Ranee's exile and persecution, and the unjust treatment of Chuttur Singh,—no Sirdar or person of importance would have been led astray by the unpremeditated outrage of Mooltan. For five months the revolt made no progress. In the sixth month the defection of Rajah Shere Singh and the suspension of operations at Mooltan turned the scale against prudent counsels and gave redoubled force to fanaticism and ambition. Measures for which the British Resident and the Governor-General were solely responsible, made a hero out of the timid Dewan Moolraj, a martyr out of the baffled Maharanee, and a formidable rebel leader out of the infirm and aged Governor, Sirdar Chuttur Singh.

Lord Dalhousie could not, or would not, see, that his full responsibility, not only for the military delays, but for every exciting and irritating incident, and for every step, good or bad, that was taken before or after the first explosion at Mooltan, effectually barred his ingenious method of separating the Durbar, as "the Government of Lahore", from the Resident, the absolute head of that Government. During the period prescribed by the Treaty for the Maharajah's minority, no crisis, no second struggle, could absolve the British Government from the obligations of Guardianship and management, so long as it professed to fulfil those duties, and was able to do so without interruption.

Even supposing that every administrative measure before the outbreak at Mooltan, and every step taken by the Resident after it, had been the wisest possible,—supposing the rebellion had not been in the slightest degree provoked or extended by any error, excess, omission, or delay of the British Government,—Lord Dalhousie's case would not be in the least improved. Supposing that the surmise by which he attempted to justify the annexation, were demonstrably true, and that the Sikhs were really animated, from the first day of the occupation, with so deep and bitter a hostility, that they only watched their opportunity for revolt, and would never have been pacified without a second lesson, then I say that they were entitled to that second lesson without any extra charge. The State of Lahore had paid heavily in money, and in territory, for the first lesson; and we had undertaken, in consideration of an annual subsidy, secured on the public revenues administered by ourselves, to perform the office of Teacher for a term of years. If unexpected difficulties had presented themselves in the performance of this office, we should, even then, have had no right to complain. But it was not so. We understood quite well the nature of the evils we had engaged to encounter and cure, and they were clearly aggravated by our own malpractice.

In his last instructions to the Resident, before publicly announcing the annexation of the Punjaub to the British dominions, Lord Dalhousie wrote as follows:—

> "The time has arrived at which it is necessary that the determination which the Governor-General has formed regarding the future administration of the Punjaub, should be communicated to *the Government at Lahore*.
>
> "On meeting *the Council of Regency*, you will present to them the Note herewith transmitted, in which the determination of the Government of India, regarding our future relations with the Punjaub, is fully set forth.
>
> "*If the Government of Lahore* should acquiesce in that determination, you are authorised to grant the Terms which are contained in the enclosed paper."*

Lord Dalhousie's object in thus thrusting prominently forward the throttled Council of Regency, and investing it, in its last agony, with the character of "the Government of Lahore", is transparently obvious. He wished to fasten upon the Regency a sort of national responsibility, in which the Maharajah might be included. But the Council of Regency, apart from British control, never was "the Government of Lahore", and its maintenance up to the date of annexation, proves the very contrary of what Lord Dalhousie wanted. The continued existence of this Regency, throughout the rebellion, proves that British responsibility and Guardianship were never

* *Papers, Punjaub*, 1849, p. 648.

shaken off or shifted for a day. If indeed the British Resident had been driven from his position at Lahore; if he had lost the custody of the Maharajah's person; if he had been forced to abdicate for a time the functions of government, and the Ward had thrown off his tutelage, the Guardian might have been justified in reentering the country as a conqueror, and declaring all previous engagements to be at an end. But no such interruption ever took place. The Resident's authority as chief ruler of the Punjaub was never suspended. During the rebellion, which in Lord Dalhousie's opinion warranted him in dethroning his Ward, the capital city was never disturbed; and the Government of the Punjaub, exactly as we had chosen to organise it,—including the Council of Regency,—was unaltered to the last. Six, if not seven,* out of the eight Councillors remained faithful to their engagements, and six of them signed the Terms, under compulsion.†

These six Sirdars,—Rajah Deena Nath, Rajah Tej Singh, Bhaee Nidhan Singh (the head of the Sikh religion), Fakeer Noor-ood-deen, Shumshere Sing Sindhanwalla, and Uttur Sing Kaleewalla,—who were perfectly blameless in their public conduct,—were told that "if they refused to accept the Terms which the Governor-General offered, the Maharajah and themselves would be entirely at his mercy", and would not be "entitled to receive any allowance whatever." If they signed the Terms, and continued "to give their advice and assistance, whenever they were called upon to do so", their jagheers (landed estates) would not be confiscated, though no promise of hereditary tenure could be made. But, "if they did not subscribe to the conditions", the Resident "could not promise that any consideration would be shown them."‡

In the last crisis of the rebellion, on the 18th of November, a Proclamation had been issued, sanctioned and approved by Lord Dalhousie on the 14th of December 1848, which contained the following announcement:—

* One of them, Runjore Singh Majeetia, being only suspected.

† *Papers, Punjaub*, 1849, pp. 649, 653.

‡ *Ibid.*, pp. 649, 650.

"It is not the desire of the British Government that those who are innocent of the above offences, who have taken no part, secretly or openly, in the disturbances, and who have remained faithful in their obedience to the Government of Maharajah Duleep Singh,—be they Sikh or be they of any other class,—should suffer with the guilty."*

Were the six members of the Council of Regency guilty? On the contrary, they had done their best for the British Government during a season of extraordinary trial and temptation, and had faithfully co-operated with the Resident in the administration of the Punjaub. Yet they were told that unless they signed and sealed the deposition of their Sovereign, they would be made to "suffer with the guilty", that their estates would be confiscated, that no consideration would be shown them, and that even if they took part in the destruction of the State, the hereditary tenure of their landed property would be annulled.

Was the young Maharajah Duleep Singh, whose Government was professedly upheld in this wonderful Proclamation, guilty? We must suppose that the extraordinary political casuistry of the Resident was accepted at Head Quarters, and that the Governor-General's Ward was considered to be guilty "in the person" of his mother, who was a prisoner at Benares, or of those "evil disposed and insurgent Sirdars", who, according to this document, had rebelled against his own Government. For he was made to suffer with the guilty. He was dethroned, despoiled, and banished.

Furthermore, this same Proclamation declares to "the loyal subjects of the Maharajah", as well as to any "who, merely through ignorance, may have been led away by the false statements of the evil-disposed", that "the army" of the Commander-in-Chief, Lord Gough, "has entered the Lahore territories, not as an enemy to the constituted Government, but to restore order and obedience."† But where two recent treaties stood in the way of annexation, what was a Proclamation more or less?

* *Papers, Punjaub*, p. 449. See Appendix.
† *Ibid.*, p. 449.

And though Lord Dalhousie thus publicly proclaimed on the 18th of November 1848,—confirmed in a second proclamation dated the 5th of February 1849,*—that the large army under the Commander-in-Chief was not entering the Punjaub "as an enemy to the constituted Government", he had already written secretly to the Resident, on the 3rd of October, "The Governor-General considers the State of Lahore to be, to all intents and purposes, directly at war with the British Government".†

The State of Lahore at war with the British Government, while the Sovereign of the Punjaub was at Lahore, the Ward and Pupil of the Resident! The State of Lahore at war with the British Government, while the administration of the Punjaub was carried on at Lahore by the British Resident, in the name of the infant Sovereign, by virtue of a Treaty with him, and in unaltered accordance with the arrangements of that Treaty! Where was that State of Lahore with which the British Government was at war, to be found? In the camp of Rajah Shere Singh, or in the fortress of Mooltan, which had been summoned to surrender on the 5th of September, "after the firing of a royal salute in honour of Her Majesty the Queen, and her Ally, His Highness Maharajah Duleep Singh"?‡ Was it personified by the Dewan Moolraj, or Chuttur Singh, or Shere Singh, who were all proclaimed as rebels "against the Government of Maharajah Duleep Singh"?§

Straightforward and truthful answers to these questions will prove that the British Government was not at war with the State of Lahore.

The State of Lahore in October 1848, and up to the day of its destruction, was to be found at Lahore, embodied and represented in the persons of the Maharajah, the Resident, who was at the head of the Government, and his colleagues, the Council of Regency, the continuity of whose functions was never interrupted or disturbed by rebellion, war, or tumult for a single day.

* *Papers, Punjaub*, 1849, p. 591. See Appendix.

† *Ibid.*, p. 375.

‡ *Ibid.*, p. 327; *A Year on the Punjaub Frontier*, vol. ii, p. 471.

§ *Papers, Punjaub*, 1849, pp. 260, 438, 449, 562.

Lord Dalhousie avoids altogether the question of Guardianship. He makes exaggerated complaints of universal treachery and perfidy, and founds upon them his iniquitous claims to treat the Prince, who had never ceased to be his Ally and Ward, as a vanquished enemy; to repudiate all the Treaties, which had never ceased to be enforced, as null and void; and to appropriate the Punjaub, which he had never ceased to occupy and administer in trust, as a conquest.* It was impossible for the British Government to conquer the territory, which it was occupying by virtue of a Treaty of protective alliance. Far from war having ever been declared against the State of Lahore, the war was carried on, and the submission of the rebels was demanded, from first to last, in the name of our Ally, the Maharajah Duleep Singh.

On the 3rd of October 1848, Lord Dalhousie secretly and confidentially "*intimates*" to the Resident, that he "*considers the State of Lahore to be, to all intents and purposes, directly at war with the British Government*". On the same day, he expresses his satisfaction, in another letter to the same official, at hearing that the fortress of Govindghur, in the city of Umritsur,—up to that time garrisoned by Sikh troops,—has been handed over to a British force, "*in accordance with the terms of the Treaty of Bhyrowal*".†

With a view, it may be presumed, to minimise opposition, to retain the influence of the Durbar, and the services of the local troops, and to keep the feudatory Princes and the Sikhs of our own provinces quiet, he will not openly declare war; but, with a view to ulterior demands, he "intimates" war against the Lahore Government, in a secret letter to his own agent, who is at the head of that Government!

In January 1849, three months after this secret "intimation" of war against his Ward, he desires the Ameer Dost Mahomed to be informed that "the Province of Peshawur is a portion of the territories of Maharajah Duleep Singh, and by the provisions of treaty, is subject,

* *Papers, Punjaub*, 1849, p. 661.
† *Ibid.*, p. 374. See Appendix.

during the minority of his Highness, to the control and direction of the British Government."*

Having controlled and directed the administration of the Lahore State, for two years and three months, through the troubles of a rebellion, by means of his own agent and his own nominees, in the name of his Ward and Ally, the Maharajah, under a Treaty which he upholds and enforces to the last,—he turns round when the rebellion is over, declares the Treaty to be null and void, and explains that the successful campaign, ostensibly carried on for the suppression of a rebellion against the Government of Maharajah Duleep Singh, was really a war against the Maharajah and the State of Lahore, by which the British Government has "conquered" the Punjaub.† The Blue Book reveals how this "war" was secretly and confidentially "intimated" simultaneously with a proclamation of friendship.

In his indictment against the State of Lahore, Lord Dalhousie falls into several exaggerated misstatements. He says, "the whole body of the nation,—army and people alike,—have, deliberately and unprovoked, again made war upon us".‡ In a subsequent passage of the same despatch he betrays his knowledge of the facts that "the Sikh people form comparatively a small portion of the population of the Punjaub", and that "a large proportion of the inhabitants, especially the Mahomedans", took no part in the hostilities, and had no sympathy with the rebellion.§

Even if the meaning of the phrase, "the whole body of the nation", is restricted to the dominant sect of Sikhs,—about a sixth of the population,—it is inaccurate. There is a list of thirty-four Sirdars, or leading Chieftains, in the Blue Book, who, with their relatives and dependents, took no part in the rebellion. Twenty-eight of these are Sikhs, only two are Mahomedans, and four are Hindoos. Among the six faithful members of the Council of Regency, was Bhaee Nidhan Singh, "the head of the Sikh religion".‖

Lord Dalhousie ventures to write as follows:—"It is

* *Papers, Punjaub*, 1849, p. 513. † *Ibid.*, p. 661.
‡ *Ibid.*, p. 660. § *Ibid.*, p. 664. ‖ *Ibid.*, p. 36.

a shameful fact that of the Sirdars of the State, properly so called, who signed the Treaties, the greater portion have been involved in these hostilities against us."* That also is an erroneous accusation. A careful analysis of the several lists and documents proves that the majority of those who signed the Treaties were *not* involved in hostilities against us. Of the sixteen Sirdars who signed the Treaties and Articles of Agreement of 1846, only five joined in the rebellion, and one, Runjore Singh Majeetia, who was in the Council of Regency, was imprisoned at Lahore, on suspicion of carrying on a treasonable correspondence. In the list of disaffected Sirdars, Runjore Singh Majeetia is put down as "convicted",† but his conduct was not the subject of any judicial investigation; and in another part of the Blue Book his guilt is said to have been "proved" by an attempt to escape after his arrest, and by his having destroyed or concealed some of his papers. There was nothing like evidence against him. Of the eight Councillors, then, six were faithful; one was suspected; one only, Rajah Shere Singh, took the field against the Government of Lahore.

To the list of Sirdars who remained faithful to their duty, who adhered to the cause of the Government of the Punjaub, as constituted under Treaty by the Governor-General, must certainly be added the name of Sirdar Khan Singh Mān, the Sikh Governor appointed to supersede the Dewan Moolraj, and who accompanied Mr. Vans Agnew and Lieutenant Anderson to Mooltan. So strong seems to have been the very natural prejudice against every Sikh who took part in that ill-fated expedition, that the Resident, in his first report of the treacherous destruction of the two young English officers, jumped at a hasty conclusion which was very unjust to Khan Singh Mān. He wrote to the Governor-General:—"*The Sirdar made terms for himself*; and the British officers were left to be cruelly butchered",—an account by no means borne out by the words of the only statement before him at that time. All that his informant, Peer Ibrahim Khan, the British Agent at Bhawulpore, had written on this point, was:—"Sirdar Khan Singh

* *Papers, Punjaub*, 1849, p. 660. † *Ibid.*, p. 489.

Mān, by the permission of Mr. Vans Agnew, begged for quarter, upon which he was seized, and the two gentlemen killed."

The following description of what had passed was given by an eye-witness, Kootub Shah, a Mahomedan soldier:—

"Sirdar Khan Singh offered to devote his life; but Mr. Agnew objected, saying it was useless for him to sacrifice himself; that, alone, he could do nothing; and that he had better ask for quarter. The Sirdar's people went outside the Eedgah, and demanded quarter. The troops then entered the place, and plundered everything. On their approaching the Sirdar, he said that he had asked for quarter, and that it would be useless to kill him, but that they might do what they pleased. He requested them to spare the wounded British officers. They, however, refused to listen to him, and seized him.

"During that day the Sirdar was kept in confinement in the Amkhas; the next day he was taken to the fort, *where he was put in irons with his son.*"*

This deposition was made in June 1848; and is fully confirmed by the fact, for which Sir Herbert Edwardes vouches, that "he remained in confinement throughout the siege, until the ruins of the exploded magazine at once killed and buried him. After the fall of the Fort," (in January 1849) "his body was dug out, *and was found so heavily ironed, that it must have been impossible for him to walk. His little boy had been apparently sleeping beside him on the bed.*" Major Edwardes, like the Resident, had heard conflicting accounts of Khan Singh's behaviour, but, he says, "under these circumstances, I thought it right to adopt the most charitable construction of the Sirdar's conduct, caused him to be buried with all honour, and sent the gold bangles which were on the arms of his son, to the surviving members of the family."†

Sir Herbert Edwardes likewise ascertained that Gooldeep Singh, the Sikh Commandant of the Infantry Regiment forming part of Mr. Agnew's escort, "replied alike to bribes and threats, that they might blow him away from a gun, but should never induce him to take service

* *Papers, Punjaub*, 1849, pp. 462, 463.

† *A Year on the Punjaub Frontier*, vol. ii, p. 162.

with the enemy." He, also, "was put in irons by Moolraj, and in despair at the shame which had been brought on Mr. Agnew's escort, threw himself into a well, as he was passing it under a guard, and was drowned."*

In the list of "openly disaffected Sirdars of the Lahore State, ascertained to be in rebellion and insurrection", forwarded by the Resident on the 25th of December 1848, for the information of the Governor-General, we find Golab Singh Povindea and his son Sirdar Alla Singh included, to whose names, however, with two others, this note is appended :—"It is most probable that these Sirdars are under restraint with the Peshawur troops."† They were certainly under restraint.

Sirdar Goolab Singh Povindea was the General in command of the Division of Sikh troops at Peshawur, and also Governor of the Province, and Major George Lawrence,‡ the Resident's Assistant at that place, repeatedly praises his constant exertions, and those of his son, Colonel Alla Singh, to preserve good order in the district, and keep the troops steady to their allegiance.§ Indeed all the superior officers at this station, with one exception, appear to have been most active and zealous, and to have done their best on behalf of the Government of Lahore.‖ With their assistance, Major Lawrence most gallantly remained at his post until the middle of October 1848, when the troops broke into open mutiny. Soon after this, an intercepted letter from the rebel leader, Rajah Shere Singh, contains this passage :—"The Peshawur troops have left that place, with all the guns. The Povindea" (Sirdar Golab Singh Povindea) "and Elahee Bukhsh" (the General of Artillery)¶ "are in confinement, and the Feringhees have fled to the Khyber."** Elahee Bukhsh escaped from confinement, and came into Lord Gough's camp immediately after the battle of Chillianwalla.††

* *A Year on the Punjaub Frontier*, vol. ii, p. 161.

† *Papers, Punjaub*, 1849, p. 490.

‡ Now General Sir George Lawrence.

§ *Papers, Punjaub*, 1849, pp. 291, 315, 339, 397, 398.

‖ *Ibid.*, 1849, pp. 339, 397.

¶ *Ibid.*, p. 340.

** *Ibid.*, p. 414.

†† Captain J. H. L. Archer's *Commentaries on the Punjaub Campaign* (W. H. Allen, 1878), p. 80.

Thus Lord Dalhousie's wholesale impeachment is not just, even if restricted "to the army". Again we find General Whish, in his final despatch of the 23rd January 1849, after the fall of Mooltan, expressing his thanks to General Cortlandt, "who commanded the Regular Regiments and Artillery of the Durbar"*—*i. e.* of the Lahore Government,—and the Governor-General himself sends his thanks to General Cortlandt for the same services "*as an officer of the Maharajah of Lahore*, through the Resident."†

Notwithstanding the defection of Rajah Shere Singh, Major Edwardes had still a considerable force of Durbar troops under his command at the end of the siege of Mooltan, and was able to detach six guns and a Regular Regiment, besides Irregular troops, in January 1849, to reinforce Lieutenant Taylor at Lukkee.‡ That officer and Lieutenant Young, acting under the directions of Major Edwardes, maintained themselves in different parts of the Derajàt and Trans-Indus territory, and retook several forts from the insurgents, without the aid of any British troops.§ Some of their men were the old Regular Infantry and Artillery of the Lahore Government, some were new levies, but all were in the service of the Punjaub State, and raised from the population of the country subject to Maharajah Duleep Singh. On the 19th of January 1849 Major Edwardes writes: "When Lieutenant Pearse joins Lieutenant Taylor, those two officers will have 3,300 men, twelve guns, and about twenty zumboorahs, with the fort of Lukkee in their possession as a rallying point." "As it is, I believe that Lieutenant Taylor will be able to confine the Dooranees to Bunnoo, and preserve the peace of the frontier, throughout the war, without the assistance of one regular soldier from the army of the Punjaub."‖

Lieutenant (now General Reynell) Taylor himself writes, his letter being quoted by Lord Dalhousie, in a despatch to the Secret Committee, dated February 21st, 1849: "The arrival of Lieutenant Pollock will give me

* *Papers, Punjaub*, 1849, p. 556. † *Ibid.*, p. 586.
‡ *Ibid.*, pp. 551, 570. § *Ibid.*, pp. 588, 630.
‖ *Ibid.*, p. 551; "army of the Punjaub" here means Lord Gough's army: it was officially so designated.

a disposable force of 5,000 men and twelve guns, with a strong fort, garrisoned by 500 men and 5 guns."*

Major Edwardes writes to Lieutenant Young, his letter being dated as late as "February 3rd, 1849":—

"I request that you will proceed to Hurrund, under the Soliman Range, in the district of Dera Ghazee Khan, and make a reconnoissance of the fort there, which has been held against the Maharajah by Moolraj's soldiers, since June last. Four hundred Rohillas and Punjabees, under Mayuh Doss, commandant, in the service of Misr Sahib Dyal, and the two guns of Dewan Jowahir Mull Dutt, are placed at your disposal, and will accompany you to Hurrund, with the view of assisting the irregular force now beleaguering Hurrund, in attacking the fort."†

The fort "held against the Maharajah" was attacked and taken by the Maharajah's troops, whose conduct Lieutenant Young praises. One superior officer, at least, who was with Lieutenant Young, was a Sikh,—Futteh Singh, mentioned as "a good soldier". When this fort, "held against the Maharajah", surrendered, Lieutenant Young says, "I ordered the chiefs to come first, and sent the Subadar of the Sappers' Company to receive them, an honour he deserves."‡

The troops under the command of two of the loyal Sirdars, Misr Sahib Dyal and Dewan Jowahir Mull, did good service to the end of the campaign. Dewan Jowahir Mull in person, with Sheikh Emam-ood-deen, an officer of high rank under the Lahore Government, formerly Governor of Cashmere, were present "with their men" at the action of Soorujkoond, near Mooltan, on the 7th November 1848, and are said by Major Edwardes to have "behaved very well."§ Soon after this affair, Sheikh Emam-ood-deen and his force were detached by Major Edwardes, to drive the rebels out of the district of Jhung; and while General Whish was concluding the siege of Mooltan, the Sheikh was occupied in investing the stronghold of Chuniote, the rebel garrison of which, 2,000 strong, laid down their arms to General Whish on the 9th February 1849, on his march from Mooltan to

* *Punjaub Papers*, 1849, pp. 585, 589.

† *Ibid.*, p. 631.

‡ *Ibid.*, pp. 632, 633.

§ *Ibid.*, p. 422.

join Lord Gough's army, and were made over as prisoners to Sheikh Emam-ood-deen.*

Sheikh Emam-ood-deen was actively engaged to the very end of the campaign. "On the 14th March 1849, Sirdar Chuttur Singh, Rajah Sher Singh, and the principal Sikh leaders, delivered their swords into the hands of the British General; and, at the same time, were surrendered forty-one pieces of artillery; while the remnant of the Sikh army, without provisions, with Abbott's force on their rear, the Cashmerians on their right, *Sheikh Emam-ood-deen* and Gilbert in front,—to the number of 16,000 men, laid down their arms in presence of the British troops."†

Misr Sahib Dyal, whose men, also, did their duty faithfully to the last, was selected by the Resident in November 1848, to accompany the Head-quarters of the Commander-in-Chief, Lord Gough, "as the chief officer on the part of the Durbar",—the Regency, with whom, according to Lord Dalhousie's private "intimation", we were then, "to all intents and purposes, directly at war!" He is described as "an able and highly intelligent person, of considerable experience and knowledge of the country, and of approved fidelity to the interests of the young Maharajah and the British Government."‡

This same Misr Sahib Dyal had, at an earlier period, brought to a successful conclusion, by means of the troops under his own command, a most important affair, which had caused much anxiety to the Resident, and occupied a large British force for more then a month,—the destruction and dispersion of a formidable band of insurgents, at one time 5,000 in number, under a noted fanatic, Bhaee Maharaj Singh, who, in communication with Dewan Moolraj, the rebel Governor of Mooltan, and well provided with funds, was scouring the country, and summoning the Sikhs to join in a religious war. The last scene in the active career of this fanatic is thus

* *Papers, Punjaub*, 1849, pp. 457, 584; Edwardes's *Year on the Punjaub Frontier*, vol. ii, p. 556.

† *Commentaries on the Punjaub Campaign*, by Capt. J. H. L. Archer (W. H. Allen, 1878).

‡ *Papers, Punjaub*, 1849, p. 444.

described in the Resident's despatch of the 13th June 1848.

"Misr Sahib Dyal was as good as his word; and he and his people kept their promise faithfully. On arriving at Jhung, the Bhaee's force had diminished to about 1000 or 1200 men; the Misr's party immediately attacked them, and, though really inferior in numbers, they were fresh, while their opponents were hungry, and tired by a long and harassing retreat. A great many of the rebels were killed in the encounter, and three or four of the Misr's men, and ten or twelve wounded. The whole rebel force was driven into the Chenab, a difficult river to cross at all times, and now formidable from being much swollen by the rains and the melted snow. It is calculated that from 500 to 600, horse and foot, perished in the river,—among the rebels, Bhaee Maharaj. Three hundred of the rebels were taken by the Misr's soldier's in boats, and put into confinement in Jhung. The Bhaee's four officers, Sikhs of some note, were among the prisoners, and are now on their way to Lahore in irons."*

Lord Dalhousie writes to the Secret Committee that "the destruction of the outlaw, Bhaee Maharaj, and the utter discomfiture of his followers, is an event which has greatly tended to the support of British authority."†

The death of Bhaee Maharaj on that occasion became a matter of doubt;‡ but his fame and influence were annihilated; and Lord Dalhousie, in his final Minute, declaring the annexation of the Punjaub, admits that "the measures taken against Bhaee Maharaj Singh, who, with some thousand followers was raising the country in the Rechna Doab, and the flight and dispersion of his followers, combined to keep down any manifestations of disaffection in the neighbourhood of Lahore."§

Thus even his own words, extracted from the Blue Book, contradict Lord Dalhousie's complaint that "the Regency, during these troubles, gave no substantial or effective assistance to the British Government."||

It is true that the Resident at one time speaks of his Councillors as merely "acquiescing" in the plans he was

* *Papers, Punjaub*, 1849, p. 213.

† *Ibid.*, p. 187.

‡ *Ibid.*, p. 625. Bhaee Maharaj was, in fact, afterwards captured, taken with Moolraj to Calcutta, and transported to Singapore in June 1850.

§ *Ibid.*, p. 657.

|| *Ibid.*, p. 660.

pursuing,—as deficient in "zeal, energy, and judgment".* On the 14th July 1848, however, he writes :—" A great change has come over the spirit of the Durbar : they have been making the most decided and very successful exertions to procure carriage of every description for the use of the British troops, and to aid in the conveyance of the siege train."† One member of the Regency, Rajah Deena Nath, was sent from Lahore on a mission into the Hazara Province in September 1848; and after his return the Resident writes to the Governor-General :—

"His presence in that part of the country had the effect of assuring the inhabitants, and he certainly appears to have used his influence, in every way, to defeat the machinations of Sirdar Chuttur Singh. Since his return he appears to have entered, zealously and earnestly, into the measures adopted for punishing the rebels, by the confiscation of their jaghires, and the attachment of their houses and property, and for counteracting the plots of the insurgents."‡

On August 16th, 1848 the Resident writes as follows to Lord Dalhousie : "The conduct of the Durbar, collectively and individually, has been entirely satisfactory in everything connected with this outbreak, and, indeed, in all other respects for the last two months."§

Lord Dalhousie, always overlooking the fact that the control of the finances was in the hands of the British Resident, places first and foremost among the " gross violations" of Treaties of which " the Sikhs" had been guilty, the non-payment of our military subsidy.

" In return for the aid of British troops, they bound themselves to pay to us a subsidy of 22 lakhs per annum. From the day when the Treaty was signed, to the present hour, not one rupee has ever been paid. Loans advanced by the British Government to enable them to discharge the arrears of their disbanded troops have never been repaid."||

And in the Proclamation declaring the Punjaub to have become British territory, he says :—" Of their annual tribute no portion whatever has at any time been paid ; and large loans, advanced to them by the Government of India, have never been repaid."†

* *Papers, Punjaub*, 1849, p. 197.
† *Ibid.*, p. 256.
‡ *Ibid.*, p. 379.
§ *Ibid.*, p. 289.
|| *Ibid.*, p. 659.
¶ *Ibid.*, p. 654.

The Blue Book contradicts the assertion that "not one rupee", that "no portion", had ever been paid. On February 23rd, 1848, the Resident reports as follows to the Governor-General. "The Durbar have paid into this treasury gold to the value of Rupees 1,356,837. By this payment they have reduced their debt to the British Government from upwards of forty lakhs of rupees to less than twenty-seven."*

In this same despatch, written about six weeks before the outbreak at Mooltan, the Resident recorded his satisfaction with the financial arrangements and prospects of the Durbar.

"They have thus, by economy and care, been able to make good four months' pay of the Irregular Cavalry, to discharge the whole of the arrears of the men who have been pensioned and disbanded, to meet their current expenses, and have still, at this moment, full eight lakhs of rupees in the different treasuries to meet the public exigencies."†

If a financial equilibrium had not been restored, and if the regular payment of the tribute had not commenced, when the rebellion of 1848 once more threw everything into confusion, it was no fault of the Council of Regency. Not only had the British authorities accepted the trust with their eyes open to the disordered state of the finances, but the Resident—opposed by the Council of Regency and supported by the Governor-General,—had introduced extensive changes into the fiscal system, leading, as had been anticipated, to a very serious loss of revenue, which he fully admits in his reports to the Governor-General on August 28th, and December 16th, 1847, and January 12th, 1848.‡

All these measures received the Governor-General's approval and confirmation. They were not favourably viewed by the Council of Regency, but no opposition was attempted, or would have been permitted. The Resident makes the following remarks in a despatch to Lord Dalhousie of April 6th, 1848.

* *Papers, Punjaub*, 1849, pp. 110, 111.

† *Ibid.*, p. 111.

‡ *Ibid.*, pp. 22, 23, 24, 56, 57, 93, 99, 104, 105.

"The settlement was, of course, most summary, and its details have yet to be filled up. Its working must be most carefully watched. The Durbar was averse to its introduction, but yielded, as they always do; and contented themselves, with the exception of Rajah Deena Nath, with standing aloof from its execution; leaving the whole matter to the Resident and his Assistants.

"Rajah Deena Nath sees the financial embarrassment of the State, and feels that the more we interfere with details, especially where the revenue is concerned, the less will be the Durbar's responsibility for financial difficulties and deficiences."*

There is no reason to doubt the wisdom of these revenue settlements; they prove, however, that the temporary failure of the Punjaub State to meet its pecuniary engagements was not wilful or faithless; they prove not merely the full knowledge and participation of the British Government in those fiscal and administrative changes which made immediate solvency impossible, but its sole responsibility for those changes.

Yet Lord Dalhousie places the regular payment of the Subsidy among "the main provisions of the agreement", which "the Sikhs" had "either entirely evaded, or grossly violated."† There was neither evasion nor violation. The use of such terms is positively shameful. The only cause of the subsidy having fallen into arrears, was that the Resident, in the plenitude of his powers, had thought fit to lessen the receipts of the State, and to divert the expenditure into other channels. These financial measures were, doubtless, most judicious, but they were entirely the Resident's work, approved by the Governor-General, reluctantly accepted by the Durbar. They were of temporary effect; and ample assets remained available, at the end of the war, for the gradual liquidation of all possible demands on the part of the British Government.

Lord Dalhousie totally fails to make out any violation of the Treaty against the Lahore State,—the only specific instance he adduces, the non-payment of the subsidy, being, as we have seen, a mere matter of account, by which the case is not in the least modified to the prejudice of the State of Lahore. He contrives to fasten a plausible stigma of perfidy and violation of treaties upon

* *Papers, Punjaub*, 1849, p. 128. † *Ibid.*, p. 659.

the State of Lahore, only by ringing the changes through several paragraphs, upon the terms, "the Sikh nation", "the Sikhs", "the Sikh people", and "the Government", or "State of Lahore",* until a thorough confusion is established. For these are not convertible terms.

What "the State of Lahore" was, and what "the Government of Lahore" was, during the British occupation and management, under the Treaty of Bhyrowal, we have just determined.

"The Sikh people", as we have already remarked, is not a phrase synonymous with "the people of the Punjaub", the great majority of whom took no share in the revolt, and felt no sympathy with it; while at least 20,000 subjects of the Lahore State, enrolled in its service, fought on the side of the Government, and assisted in suppressing the rebellion.

Lord Dalhousie evidently perceived the forensic and moral difficulty in the way of annexation, created by the relation of Guardianship under the Treaty of Bhyrowal, between the two States,—between the infant Sovereign of the Punjaub and the Governor-General of British India. He saw the necessity of meeting that difficulty somehow. He could not leave it entirely unnoticed. But he did not state it fully or fairly; and the solution offered in the following passages is quite inadequate.

> "It has been objected that the present dynasty in the Punjaub cannot with justice be subverted, since Maharajah Duleep Sing, being yet a minor, can hardly be held responsible for the acts of the nation. With deference to those by whom these views have been entertained, I must dissent entirely from the soundness of this doctrine."†

No such unsound doctrine lay before him. The objection was not to the subversion of a minor, but to the subversion of a Ward by his Guardian. Nor was it merely a question of "subverting a dynasty", but of subverting a State, protected and administered, under Treaty, by the British Government. I have already shown that Lord Dalhousie had no right to speak of the

* *Punjaub Papers*, 1849, pp. 661, 662.
† *Ibid.*, p. 663.

acts of the rebels, either as "the acts of the nation", or of "the State of Lahore."

Lord Dalhousie went on to argue that this imaginary false doctrine,—the irresponsibility of a minor Sovereign, —had "been disregarded heretofore, in practice, and disregarded in the case of the Maharajah Duleep Singh himself." He continues thus:—

"When, in 1845, the Khalsa army invaded our territories, the Maharajah was not held to be free from responsibility, nor was he exempted from the consequences of his people's acts. On the contrary, the Government of India confiscated to itself the richest provinces of the Maharajah's kingdom, and was applauded for the moderation which had exacted no more.

"Furthermore, the Maharajah having been made to pay the penalty of the past offences of his people, due warning was given him that he would be held, in like manner, responsible for their future acts. The Maharajah, in reply, acknowledging this warning, says, 'If, in consequence of the recurrence of misrule in my Government, the peace of the British frontier be disturbed, I should be held responsible for the same.'

"If the Maharajah was not exempted from responsibility on the plea of his tender years, at the age of eight, he cannot, on that plea, be entitled to exemption from a like responsibility, now that he is three years older."*

It is strange that Lord Dalhousie should have so completely overlooked the real difference between 1846 and 1849. The question of age was immaterial at both periods. There was no plea of exemption in 1846 when the warning was given and acknowledged, because the Maharajah was the reigning Prince of an independent State. Although he was a minor, his mother, his near relatives, and their chosen advisers, were the actual Rulers of the State. In 1849 the actual Ruler of the State was the British Resident, under the Governor-General's instructions.

Of course a minor Prince is the personal representative of the State, and must stand or fall with its fortunes. But a minor Prince under the tutelage of a powerful neighbour, cannot justly be held responsible for the acts of the nation which his Guardian has undertaken to guide and control.

* *Papers, Punjaub*, 1849, p. 663.

In 1846 the Maharajah was a conquered enemy. In 1849 the Maharajah was a Ward; the British Government was the Guardian. His mother, his natural Guardian and late Regent, was banished from the Punjaub; several of his relatives and former ministers were in prison or exile. The Maharajah was now entirely exempt from responsibility, simply because all responsibility had been assumed by the British Government.

From the 16th of December 1846, the date of the Treaty of Bhyrowal, down to the 29th of March 1849, when the Proclamation annexing the Punjaub was issued, the Government of Lahore was in strict subordination to the British Government; and its subordination was never interrupted, suspended, or relaxed for a single day. If, indeed, the Government of Lahore could justly have been made responsible for any of the untoward events of 1848 and 1849, Sir Frederick Currie, the Resident, must have been the first person indicted, for he was the absolute head of that Government. This is a fair *reductio ad absurdum* of that sophistical and fallacious rhetoric, by which Lord Dalhousie confounded "the Sikhs", "the Sikh nation", "the people of the Punjaub", "the Lahore Government", and "the State of Lahore", as if they were synonymous and co-extensive terms, with the object of justifying the violation of Treaties, and the evasion of a sacred duty.

Lord Dalhousie's motives, as avowed by himself, for abandoning the office of Guardian, and the noble work of restoring order and self-government to the Punjaub State, when so much progress had already been secured, were not of the highest order. To me they appear morally low, politically short-sighted, and altogether unworthy of a great and generous nation, claiming to play the part of Imperial Instructor and Exemplar to India and the East. He argued that if our Government continued to maintain "the Sikh nation as an independent State", and instituted a reformed administration by "a larger measure of British control", "we should have all the labour, all the anxiety, all the responsibility, which would attach to the territories if they were actually made our own; while we should not reap the corresponding benefits of increase of revenue and acknowledged possession."*

That labour, anxiety, and responsibility we had undertaken; those benefits,—imaginary enough, as we now know,—we had foregone by the Treaty of Bhyrowal. As to "a larger measure of British control", there could be no larger measure than those "unlimited powers" which we held under that Treaty, and which the Resident had never ceased to exercise.

On the other hand, Lord Dalhousie observed, "the revenues are very considerable in the aggregate. A large proportion has, hitherto, been diverted from the public treasury in jaghires to the Chiefs. A considerable amount of revenue will now be recovered from the confiscation of the jaghires of those who have been engaged in hostilities against us."† He has "no hesitation in expressing a confident belief that the Punjaub will, at no distant time, be not only a secure, but a profitable possession."‡

"At no distant time",—before Lord Dalhousie's tour of office expired,—this "confident belief" was signally contradicted.

In addition to this delusive hope of profit, and the desire to evade a burdensome obligation, Lord Dalhousie alleges a regard for "self-defence", and "the security of our own territories", as compelling us "to relinquish the policy which would maintain the independence of the Sikh nation in the Punjaub."§

"There never will be peace in the Punjaub", he urges, "so long as its people are allowed to retain the means and the opportunity of making war. There never can be now any guaranty for the tranquillity of India, until we shall have effected the entire subjection of the Sikh people, and destroyed its power as an independent nation."||

The same equivocal use of the terms, "the Sikh people" or "nation", and "the people of the Punjaub", is employed here, as throughout this despatch. The people of the Punjaub in general were not hostile, as Lord Dal-

* *Papers, Punjaub*, 1849, pp. 662, 663.

† *Ibid.*, p. 664.

‡ *Ibid.*, p. 665.

§ *Ibid.*, p. 661.

|| *Ibid.*, p. 662.

housie acknowledged. The Sikh army and the turbulent portion of the Sikh people, had been effectually subjected, and deprived of the means of making war. Reduced in numbers, subdued to orderly discipline, the Sikh army never could have regained its insolent preeminence in the State, as the embodied representative of the Sikh religion and Commonwealth,—the Khalsa Punth. And its conspicuous humiliation was sure to operate in a very wholesome manner upon the Sikh population, not only in the Punjaub, but throughout Sirhind, the Jullundhur Doab, and the feudatory States on both sides of the Sutlej.

Deprived of all supremacy and influence over many of these minor States, whose resources were now transferred to the British Government, and proved of material assistance during the campaign of 1849, weakened by the loss of Jullundhur and Cashmere,—the former in our possession, the latter placed on her flank as a jealous rival,—the Punjaub State, even if freed from the British occupation, could hardly be considered independent after the Treaties of 1846. Certainly her independence was not of such a character as to afford reasonable grounds of apprehension for "the tranquillity of India", or for "the security of our own territories." Lord Hardinge had taken good care of that.

By Articles II, III, and IV, of the Treaty of the 9th of March 1846, the Maharajah Duleep Singh renounced for himself, his heirs and successors, "all claim to, or connection with the territories to the south of the Sutlej", and between the rivers Sutlej and Beas (the Jullundhur Doab), ceded to the British Government; and also gave up Cashmere and the Hill Countries, designed to form a Principality for Rajah Golab Singh. By Article VII, the "Regular Army of the Lahore State" was "henceforth limited to twenty-five Battalions of Infantry, and 12,000 Cavalry", and this force was never to be increased without the express permission of the British Government. By Article IX, the control of the rivers Beas, Sutlej, and Indus, in respect to tolls and ferries, was to rest with the British Government. By Article X, British troops, due notice being given, were to be allowed to pass through the Lahore territories. By Article XI, no European or American was to be taken into the service of the Punjaub State without the permission of the British Government. By Articles XII and XIII, "the independent Sovereignty" of Rajah Golab Singh was recognised, and any dispute or difference between him and the Lahore State was to be referred to the British Government, whose decision was to be final. By Article XIV, no territorial acquisitions were henceforth to be made "without the concurrence of the British Government."*

The "independence" stipulated in this Treaty for Rajah Golab Singh, tributary and feudatory of the British Government, signifies, of course, merely independence of Lahore. This is an instance of the looseness and want of precision with which the terms "independent" and "independence" have been used in our Indian Treaties and State papers, and by no one more frequently than Lord Dalhousie. But even if the meaning of the term "independence", which he applies to "the Sikh nation", be confined to that freedom of internal administration which was to be restored to the Punjaub at the end of the Maharajah's minority, there certainly was nothing in the prospect to alarm a British statesman.

Lord Dalhousie, in fact, could not have constructed his specious case of "self-defence" against the dangerous "independence" of the Punjaub State,—he could not even have deceived himself on the subject,—if he had not employed that misleading formula, "the independence of the Sikh nation."

The Sikh nation,—if a sect can be called a nation,—neither constitutes the population of the Punjaub, nor is confined to the Punjaub. It was not the Sikh religion, nor the Sikh nationality within the Punjaub, that rendered the establishment of a strong and orderly Government in that country so difficult, but the large floating population of recently disbanded soldiers, and their favourite leaders, belonging to the dominant sect, and

* *Papers, the Late Hostilities*, 1846, pp. 99, 101 ; and *Collection of Treaties*, Calcutta (London: Longman and Co.), vol. ii, pp. 261, 263.

accustomed to political supremacy. The organisation of the Sikh army was not thoroughly broken up; the defeated Khalsa had not forgotten their old habits, nor lost their old hopes. All that they wanted was that second lesson, which we had promised to administer, if necessary.

Sir Henry Lawrence, the man of all others best qualified to judge, did not believe that the Sikhs had taken the lead in the outbreak of 1849. In an article on "Army Reform", which he contributed to the *Calcutta Review* of September 1856,—ten months before his own glorious death in the Lucknow Residency, beleaguered by rebels,—he warned us that there would be more enmity against us in the peaceably annexed Oude than there had been in the "conquered" Punjaub. "Proportionally few of the instigators of opposition in Lahore, and in the Sikh army", said he, "were Sikhs. They were British subjects, many of them British deserters. The general feeling of the Sikhs was hardly hostile. Many of the Sikhs were friendly,—decidedly so, compared with the Hindustanis in the Punjaub service."

Sir Henry Lawrence was strongly opposed to the annexation of the Punjaub. "He acted in the best faith for the interest of both Governments", said one who knew him well, defending him from the charge of having prepared the way for the change of rule, "and so far from desiring the annexation of the country, on finding that it could not be avoided, and that all his efforts to uphold the Native Government were unavailing, Sir Henry Lawrence was only prevented from resigning his high position, and returning to his Regiment as a Captain of Artillery, at the earnest entreaty of his friends."*

The pacification of the Punjaub after 1849, is not in the least explained by its becoming a British Province, but by the simple fact that the soldiers of Runjeet Singh's old army had been well beaten, and that they knew it. Whatever doubt may have been left on their minds after the campaign of 1846, was now effectually dispelled. They could not contend against the British

* Ferrier's *Caravan Journies* (Murray, 1856). Note by Sir John Login, p. 359.

Government. They had been made to lay down their arms; they had lost all their guns; their proudest and most trusted Chieftains were all discomfited; their saints and prophets were all discredited; their union was dissolved. They had been defeated without disgrace; a great deal of fanatical nonsense had probably been knocked out of them; and, by all accounts, they bore no particular grudge against us for the lesson we had taught them.

There is, in fact, no reason to doubt that the Punjaub would have been as peaceful and friendly under a Native Prince, as the States of Nepaul and Gwalior have been, the former for fifty years since its last defeat, the latter for twenty-four years since its final subjection to the British Government.

The Nepaulese, animated by a long career of conquest, and with an overweening confidence in their own power and resources, made war upon us in 1814. Their successes against our troops in the first campaign induced them to protract the contest for nearly two years; but they were taught the error of trusting in the inaccessibility of their mountain fastnesses, and their Envoy was compelled to present on his knees, at the British General's Durbar,* the Treaty of peace ratified by the Maharajah, giving up all the points in dispute, and ceding a large tract of territory. Since this humiliation in March 1816, a British Resident has been constantly at the capital of Nepaul; that Government has maintained the most amicable relations with us; and in 1857-8 a force of 20,000 Goorkhas, commanded by the Prime Minister and Commander-in-Chief, Maharajah Jung Bahadoor, cooperated with Lord Clyde's army in suppressing the rebellion in Oude.

The military operations of 1843 in the territories of Maharajah Scindia of Gwalior, had for their pretext and object the coercion of a turbulent and unmanageable army, unnecessarily large for the purposes of the Native State, and massed so as to threaten our frontier near the important city of Agra. Two battles were fought;

* Prinsep's *Marquis of Hastings' Administration* (Allen, 1825), vol. i, p. 205.

the defeated army was disbanded, and reorganised on a limited scale under a new and more stringent Treaty. Since that time the State of Gwalior has given no ground of complaint; and in the crisis of 1857, Maharajah Scindia and his ministers, though placed in the vortex of insurrection, surrounded by mutinous and clamorous troops,—the Gwalior Contingent,—"raised, paid, disciplined, and" (recently) "commanded by British officers", in the style which, in Lord Dalhousie's opinion, could alone make Native troops safe* —contrived to render most valuable services to the British Government. These were the prescient words of Sir Henry Lawrence, published ten years before the rebellion of 1857 :—"By Lord Ellenborough's arrangements, Gwalior is now an armed friend."† If Lord Dalhousie had not despoiled our Ward, we should have had a more efficient "armed friend" at Lahore.

Every historical analogy, every contemporaneous event, all the probabilities of the case, indicate that the Sikhs, under the reformed Government of Maharajah Duleep Singh, would have been as proud and as eager to cooperate with British troops in 1857, as were the Sikhs under the Sikh Rajahs of Puttiala, Jheend, Nabha, and Kuppoorthulla, as were the troops of the Rajah of Cashmere, or the Nepaulese under Jung Bahadoor. Delhi was the accursed city of the Mogul, the centre of Mussulman arrogance, the place of martyrdom of the great Sikh prophets, and devoted by their predictions to the vengeance of their disciples. Animated by these traditional animosities, with the hope of plunder, and "the old scorn for the Poorbeah Sepoy",‡ the Sikhs rallied to our banner in the newly raised Punjaubee Regiments, and pressed towards Delhi with confidence and good will. But these notorious inducements would have operated with double force under the rule of their own Rajah.

Lord Dalhousie argued, that "warlike in character, and long accustomed to conquest, the Sikhs must, of

* *Punjaub Papers*, 1849, p. 662.

† Sir Henry Lawrence's *Essays*.

‡ Trotter's *History of India from* 1844 *to* 1862, vol. ii, p. 70.

necessity, detest the British as their conquerors."* But if the administration of the Punjaub during the Rajah's minority had been continued, there would have been no "conquerors" to detest. It was Lord Dalhousie who converted our protective occupation into a so-called conquest. If the Treaty had not been thus violated, the defeated insurgents would have been simply a vanquished party in the State, and vanquished, as I believe, finally, by the help of another party. No humiliation would have fallen on the Maharajah, upon the Board of Regency, or upon the principal Sirdars, their followers, and the 20,000 troops, who had supported the constituted authorities. And even for the vanquished party, if the Punjaub State had been maintained, the participation of the Maharajah's army in the military exploits of the British Government, would have tempered the sting of defeat.

The fact is that the Sikh Government of the Punjaub, so long as there was a regular Government, never had the least inclination to go to war with us. The State of Lahore, throughout the time of its greatest pride and prosperity, under Runjeet Singh, had remained on the best terms with the British Government. Even after the great Maharajah's death, amid the excitement of our disasters in Affghanistan, and the operations to retrieve them and withdraw our troops, amicable relations were preserved for several years, until what Lord Hardinge correctly described as "a democratic revolution",† threw all the strength of the State into the hands of the army. The military Punchayuts used their power in a manner that was most offensive and alarming to all adherents of Runjeet Singh's dynasty. They "issued their orders, under the designation belonging to the Sikh sect before Runjeet Singh became a monarch, viz. :—the Khalsa Punth, (Khalsajee-ka Punth)"—the Company of the Elect. "They formally assumed the Government, and sent letters bearing their seal, inscribed merely with the name of God, to all local officers, military leaders, and members of the Durbar, requiring their presence and

* *Papers, Punjaub*, 1849, p. 662.

† *Papers, the late Hostilities, etc.*, 1846, p. 6.

obedience."* The Princes, the ministers, the nobles, "the head of the Sikh religion", even the superior officers of the army, all who had anything to lose, were on the side of peace with us, and good order within their own frontier. It was so in 1845, and equally, or more so, in 1849.

We have seen how long, and how stoutly, Rajah Shere Singh resisted the growing impulse,—under what an imperative summons, amid what confusion and despair, he at last yielded. And, after all, he alone, out of the eight leading Sirdars of the Punjaub, selected to form the Council of Regency, took part in the insurrection,—and then, not as a voluntary participator in the common cause, but reluctantly and hopelessly, closely touched by special motives of personal honour, and the Oriental sense of implicit filial obedience.

Many of the Sirdars withstood for a long time every incentive to rebellion, and were at last dragged or forced into it by the soldiery who surrounded them. The arrogant rapacity of Sikh domination in the army, was, in fact, the sole obstacle to be overcome before a reformed and self-sustaining Government could be established in the Punjaub. Under our protective management,—with or without a second struggle,—that obstacle would have been overcome. The reorganisation of the army, and pacification of the warlike tribes, were merely matters of time. The interval of the Rajah's minority would probably have been sufficiently long. The negotiators of the Treaty of Bhyrowal certainly contemplated the possibility of a second struggle. Lord Hardinge and Sir Henry Lawrence were prepared for it, though they did not expect it; and but for a strange succession of mishaps and errors of judgment, I firmly believe the second struggle would have been avoided. In either case, whether the second struggle was unavoidable, whether it was provoked or aggravated by our shortcomings or faults, we ought to have borne the brunt of it without complaining. There may have been a little more trouble than we liked, a little more than we looked for, but there was no more than we had bargained for.

* *Papers, the late Hostilities, etc.*, 1846, p. 8.

The spirits, the habits, the traditional pride of the old Khalsa troops, in the ranks of the local army, and in the districts chiefly inhabited by the Sikhs, were the unruly elements we had undertaken to curb and coerce. It was our duty to conquer those unruly elements; but having done so, we had no right to say, as Lord Dalhousie did, that we had "conquered" the territories under our tutelage. That was not a true conquest,—it was a breach of trust. We availed ourselves to the utmost, and to the last moment, of our advantageous position as the civil and military administrators of the Punjaub; we held its strongholds, and disposed of all its resources, including 20,000 soldiers recruited from its population; we disarmed many wavering and doubtful opponents by appealing to their conservative interests and loyal sentiments, by professing to uphold the Treaties, and disavowing hostility to their Sovereign and institutions;—all this we were authorised and bound to do, with the object of quelling the insurrection, but not with the object of violating the Treaties, as soon as the crisis was over, by turning our occupation into possession.

I have left undiscussed the secondary question, whether we may not have had some equitable claims to compensation and additional safeguards, on account of the excessive expenses, and special difficulties of quelling the revolt. Without admitting that such claims would have been well founded, it is enough to say that all our demands under those heads could have been easily secured without the annexation of the Kingdom that had been entrusted to our charge. The annexation gave us neither pecuniary compensation nor military safeguard, but set up a constant drain upon our purse, a constant strain upon our sword-arm.

The results of that ill-advised acquisition, up to the present time, seem to me to have been of a mixed character,—absolutely injurious and exhausting to the British Empire, relatively beneficial in some respects, prejudicial in others, to the people of the Punjaub,—but I can perceive no advantage, material or moral, that has been gained by any person or class, that could not have been more fully and effectually conferred and secured without annexation than with it.

Lord Dalhousie objected, that "hesitation on our part would be attributed, not to forbearance, but to fear; it would be regarded, not as the result of a magnanimous policy, but as the evidence of a pusillanimous spirit",* a most frivolous and unstatesmanlike objection. Magnanimity after success never presents the appearance of fear, and is not in the least liable to be mistaken for it. All India was thoroughly impressed with the complete subjection of the Sikh army. There were manifold means available for making that subjection, and the submission of the entire people, a visible object to the whole Peninsula, and for turning it to the honour and credit of the Imperial Power. According to Oriental ideas the greatest Sovereign is he who can make Princes, and who has the largest number of Princes under his command and protection. Lord Dalhousie might have gained the hearts of Princes and people by a plain statement of what had been done, and what it was intended to do in the Punjaub. Instead of doing so, he violated Treaties, abused a sacred trust, threw away the grandest opportunity ever offered to the British Government of planting solid and vital reform up to the Northern limits of India, and by an acquisition as unjust as it was imprudent, weakened our frontier, scattered our military strength, and entailed a heavy financial burden upon the Empire. That, I believe, will be the verdict of posterity and history upon the transactions which have just passed under our review.

‡ *Papers, Punjaub*, 1849, p. 664.

APPENDIX.

(A.)

(*Pages* 61 *to* 65.)

The dates of the following documents and extracts must be marked and observed.

The Secretary to the Government of India to the Resident at Lahore.

"Fort William, October 3, 1848.

"As may have been anticipated by you, from the earnest desire expressed by the Government, from the earliest communication made to you, after the commencement of the rebellion at Mooltan, that the fortress of Govindgurh should, in accordance with the terms of the Treaty of Bhyrowal, be occupied by British troops, the Governor-General in Council is perfectly satisfied with the intelligence now communicated to him."

The Secretary to the Government of India to the Resident at Lahore.

"Fort William, October 3, 1848.

"I am desired to intimate to you, that the Governor-General in Council considers the State of Lahore to be, to all intents and purposes, directly at war with the British Government; and he expects that those who may be, directly or indirectly, concerned in these proceedings, will be treated accordingly, by yourself and your officers."—(*Punjaub Papers*, 1849, pp. 374, 375.)

The Resident at Lahore to the Secretary with the Governor-General.

"Lahore, December 2, 1848.

"The Commander-in-Chief had crossed the Ravee; misrepresentations of the purposes of the British Government were being sedulously circulated by the disaffected; and those whose interests are on the side of the British supremacy in the Punjaub, were urgent with me, as to the expediency of putting forth some declaration to the people, which would allay the general apprehension that was felt, at the advance of the Commander-in-Chief.

"The insurgents have sent, throughout the provinces, inflammatory papers, in which they style themselves the United Khalsa, the loyal and obedient subjects of Maharajah Duleep Sing, whom the British oppressors have imprisoned, and in which they declare that the object of the British Government is the wholesale extermination of the Sikhs indiscriminately, and the suppression of the Khalsa religion.

"There is nothing too extravagant for the common people of India to believe, if it is told them by their priests and the Sirdars; the report that the offences of the rebels were to be visited on the Sikh population at large, was gaining extensive credit, and the insurgent leaders were, on this account, gaining the sympathies of many, and extensive additions to their ranks, which they would, otherwise, have been without.

"I considered it, therefore, necessary to counteract their machinations at once, by a declaration to the people of the Punjaub, of the real object of the present advance of the British army."

Now let us hear "the real object", according to the proclamation.

Proclamation by the Resident at Lahore.

"November 18, 1848.

"To the subjects, servants, and dependents of the Lahore State, and the residents, of all classes and castes, whether Sikh, Mussulman, or other, within the territories of Maharajah Duleep Sing, from the Beas to the mountains beyond Peshawur. Whereas certain evil-disposed persons and traitors, have excited rebellion and insurrection, and have seduced portions of the population of the Punjaub from their allegiance, and have raised an armed opposition to the British authority; and whereas the condign punishment of the insurgents is necessary; therefore, the British army, under the command of the Right Honourable the Commander-in-Chief, has entered the Punjaub districts. The army will not return to its cantonments, until the full punishment of all insurgents has been effected, all armed opposition to constituted authority put down, and obedience and order have been re-established.

"And whereas it is not the desire of the British Government that those who are innocent of the above offences, who have taken no part, secretly or openly, in the disturbances, and who have remained faithful in their obedience to the government of Maharajah Duleep Sing, be they Sikh, or be they of any other class, should suffer with the guilty; therefore, all persons who are not concerned, directly or indirectly, in the present disturbances, are assured that they have nothing to fear from the coming of the British army. Such persons are exhorted to remain, without apprehension, in their villages and homes, and, as loyal subjects of the Maharajah, to give every aid by providing carriage, supplies, and the like, to the army which has entered the Lahore territories, not as an enemy to the constituted Government, but to restore order and obedience. Furthermore, all classes of the community, be they Sikh, or be they of any other caste or tribe, who, merely through ignorance, may have been led away, by the false statements of the evil-disposed and insurgent Sirdars and others, and have left their homes, and assembled themselves under the standard of rebellion, are hereby admonished instantly to separate themselves from the insurgents, and to return to their villages. If they do so now, without hesitation or delay, no injury will happen to them; if they neglect this warning and advice, certain destruction will come upon them, in common with the other insurgents and rebels, and disturbers of the public peace."

Inclosure 9 in No. 42.

The Secretary with the Governor-General to the Resident at Lahore.

"Camp, Sirhind, December 14, 1848.

"The Governor-General approves of your having issued this proclamation."—(*Punjaub Papers*, 1849, pp. 448, 449.)

The Previous Proclamation Confirmed.

Extract of Proclamation by the Resident at Lahore, under orders from the Governor-General.

"Lahore Residency, February 5, 1849.

"A proclamation was issued by Sir Frederick Currie, on the 18th of November last. I now, *again*, make known, by order of the Governor-General, the terms on which alone pardon may still be obtained."—*Punjaub Papers*, 1849, p. 591.)

(B.)

THE TIMES, *Thursday, August* 31, 1882.

"THE CLAIMS OF AN INDIAN PRINCE.

"TO THE EDITOR OF THE TIMES.

"SIR,—As the era of doing justice and restoration appears to have dawned, judging from the recent truly liberal and noble act of the present Liberal Government, headed, by now, the great Gladstone the Just, I am encouraged to lay before the British nation, through the medium of *The Times*, the injustice which I have suffered, in the hope that, although generosity may not be lavished upon me to the same extent as has been bestowed upon King Cetewayo, yet that some magnanimity might be shown towards me by this great Christian Empire.

"When I succeeded to the throne of the Punjaub I was only an infant, and the Khalsa soldiery, becoming more and more mutinous and overbearing during both my uncle's and my mother's Regencies, at last, unprovoked, crossed the Sutlej and attacked the friendly British Power, and was completely defeated and entirely routed by the English Army.

"Had, at that time, my dominions been annexed to the British territories, I would have now not a word to say, for I was at that time an independent Chief at the head of an independent people, and any penalty which might have been then inflicted would have been perfectly just; but that kind, true English gentleman, the late Lord Hardinge, in consideration of the friendship which had existed between the British Empire and the 'Lion of the Punjaub', replaced me on my throne, and the diamond Koh-i-noor on my arm, at one of the Durbars. The Council of Regency, which was then created to govern the country during my minority, finding that it was not in their power to rule the Punjaub unaided, applied for assistance to the representative of the British Government, who, after stipulating for absolute power to control every Government department, entered into the Bhyrowal Treaty with me, by which was guaranteed that I should be protected on my throne until I attained the age of sixteen years, the British also furnishing troops both for the above object and preservation of peace in the country, in consideration of a certain sum to be paid to them annually by my Durbar, for the maintenance of that force.

"Thus the British nation, with open eyes, assumed my guardianship, the nature of which is clearly defined in a proclamation subsequently issued by Lord Hardinge's orders on the 20th of August 1847, which declares that the tender age of the Maharajah Duleep

Singh causes him to feel the interest of a father in the education and guardianship of the young Prince.—(*Vide* Punjaub Papers at the British Museum.)

"Two English officers carrying letters bearing my signature were despatched by the British Resident, in conjunction with my Durbar, to take possession of the fortress of Mooltan and the surrounding district in my name, but my servant, Moolraj, refusing to acknowledge my authority, caused them to be put to death, whereupon both the late Sir F. Currie and the brave Sir Herbert Edwardes most urgently requested the Commander-in-Chief of the British forces at Simla, as there were not sufficient English soldiers at Lahore at the time, to send some European troops without delay in order to crush this rebellion in the bud, as they affirmed that the consequences could not be calculated which might follow if it were allowed to spread; but the late Lord Gough, with the concurrence of the late Marquis of Dalhousie, refused to comply with their wishes, alleging the unhealthiness of the season as his reason for doing so.

"My case at that time was exactly similar to what the Khedive's is at this moment; Arabi being, in his present position, to his master what Moolraj was to me—viz., a rebel.

"At last, very tardily, the British Government sent troops (as has been done in Egypt) to quell the rebellion, which had by that time vastly increased in the Punjaub, and who entered my territories, headed by a proclamation, issued by Lord Dalhousie's orders, to the following effect:—

"'Inclosure No. 8 in No. 42.—To the subjects, servants, and dependents of the Lahore State, and residents of all classes and castes, whether Sikhs, Mussulmans, or others within the territories of Maharajah Duleep Singh. . . . . Whereas certain evil-disposed persons and traitors have excited rebellion and insurrection, and have seduced portions of the population of the Punjaub from their allegiance, and have raised an armed opposition to the British authority; and whereas the condign punishment of the insurgents is necessary, . . . therefore the British Army, under the command of the Right Hon. the Commander-in-Chief, has entered the Punjaub districts. The army will not return to its cantonments until the full punishment of all insurgents has been effected, all opposition to the constituted authority put down, and obedience and order have been re-established.'

Thus it is clear from the above that the British Commander-in-Chief did not enter my dominions as a conqueror, nor the army to stay there, and, therefore, it is not correct to assert, as some do, that the Punjaub was a military conquest.

"'And whereas it is not the desire of the British Government that those who are innocent of the above offences, who have taken no part, secretly or openly, in the disturbances, and who have remained faithful in their obedience to the Government of Maharajah Duleep Singh . . . . should suffer with the guilty.'

"But after order was restored, and finding only a helpless child to deal with, and the temptation being too strong, Lord Dalhousie annexed the Punjaub, instead of carrying out the solemn compact entered into by the British Government at Bhyrowal; sold almost all my personal, as well as all my private property, consisting of jewels, gold and silver plate, even some of my wearing apparel and household furniture, and distributed the proceeds, amounting (I was told) to £250,000, as prize money among those very troops who had come to put down rebellion against my authority.

"Thus I, the innocent, who never lifted up even my little finger against the British Government, was made to suffer in the same manner with my own subjects who would not acknowledge my authority, in spite of the declaration of the above-quoted Proclamation that it is not the desire of the British Government that the innocent should suffer with the guilty.

"Lord Dalhousie, in writing to the Secret Committee of the late Court of Directors, in order to justify his unjust act, among other arguments employs the following. He says:—

"'It has been objected that the present dynasty in the Punjaub cannot with justice be subverted, since the Maharajah Duleep Singh, being yet a minor, can hardly be held responsible for the acts of the nation. With deference to those by whom these views have been entertained, I must dissent entirely from the soundness of this doctrine. It is, I venture to think, altogether untenable as a principle; it has been disregarded heretofore in practice, and disregarded in the case of the Maharajah Duleep Singh. When in 1845 the Khalsa army invaded our territories, the Maharajah was not held to be free from responsibility, nor was he exempted from the consequences of the acts of the people. On the contrary, the Government of India confiscated to itself the richest provinces of the Maharajah's kingdom, and was applauded for the moderation which had exacted no more. If the Maharajah was not exempted from responsibility on the plea of his tender years at the age of eight, he cannot on that plea be entitled to exemption from a like responsibility now that he is three years older.'

"But in thus arguing, His Lordship became blind to the fact that in 1845, when the Khalsa army invaded the British territories, I was an independent chief, but after the ratification of the Bhyrowal treaty I was made the ward of the British nation; and how could I, under these circumstances, be held responsible for the neglect of my Guardians in not crushing Moolraj's rebellion at once, the necessity of doing which was clearly and repeatedly pointed out by the British Resident at Lahore?

"Again, His Lordship says: 'The British Government has rigidly observed the obligations which the treaty imposed on them, and fully acted up to the spirit and letter of its contract.' No doubt all this was or may have been true, except so far that neither peace was preserved in the country nor I protected on my throne till I attained the age of sixteen years; two very important stipulations of that treaty.

"He further alleges: 'In return for the aid of the British troops they (my Durbar) bound themselves to pay to us a subsidy of 22 lakhs (£220,000) per annum, . . . from the day when that treaty was signed to the present hour, not one rupee has ever been paid.'

"Now, the above statement is not correct, because of the following despatch which exists: 'Enclosure No. 5 in No. 23,' the Acting Resident at Lahore affirms, 'The Durbar has paid into this treasury gold to the value of Rs. 13,56,637 0*a*. 6*p*.' (£135,837 14*s*. 1*d*., taking the value of a rupee at 2*s*.)

"Likewise, Lord Dalhousie alludes to Sirdar Chuttur Singh's conduct. Enclosure 19 in No. 36 will show those who care to look for it the reprimand which Captain Abbott then received from the Resident for his treatment of that Chief, who, after that, with his sons, without doubt, believed that the Bhyrowal Treaty was not going to be carried out; and, judging from the events which followed, were they right in their views, or were they not?

"1. Thus I have been most unjustly deprived of my kingdom, yielding, as shown by Lord Dalhousie's own computation in (I think) 1850, a surplus revenue of some £500,000, and no doubt now vastly exceeds that sum.

"2. I have also been prevented, unjustly, from receiving the rentals of my private estates (*vide* Prinsep's *History of the Sikhs*, compiled for the Government of India) in the Punjaub, amounting to some £130,000 per annum, since 1849, although my private property is not confiscated by the terms of the annexation which I was compelled to sign by my guardians when I was a minor, and, therefore, I presume it is an illegal document, and I am still the lawful Sovereign of the Punjaub; but this is of no moment, for I am quite content to be the subject of my Most Gracious Sovereign, no matter how it was brought about, for her graciousness towards me has been boundless.

"3. All my personal property has also been taken from me, excepting £20,000 worth, which I was informed by the late Sir John Login was permitted to be taken with me to Futtehghur when I was exiled; and the rest, amounting to some £250,000, disposed of as stated before. What is still more unjust in my case is, that most of my servants who remained faithful to me were permitted to retain all their personal and private property, and to enjoy the rentals of their landed estates (or jagheers), given to them by me and my predecessors; whereas I, their master, who did not even lift up my little finger against the British nation, was not considered worthy to be treated on the same footing of equality with them, because, I suppose, my sin being that I happened to be the ward of a Christian power.

"The enormous British liberality permits a life stipend of £25,000 per annum, which is reduced by certain charges (known to the proper authorities) to some £13,000, to be paid to me from the revenues of India.

"Lately, an Act of Parliament has been passed by which, some months hence, the munificent sum of some £2,000 will be added to my above stated available income, but on the absolute condition that my estates must be sold at my death, thus causing my dearly-loved English home to be broken up, and compelling my descendants to seek some other asylum.

"A very meagre provision, considering of what and how I have been deprived, has also been made for my successors.

"If one righteous man was found in the two most wicked cities of the world, I pray God that at least one honourable, just, and noble Englishman may be forthcoming out of this Christian land of liberty and justice to advocate my cause in Parliament, otherwise what chance have I of obtaining justice, considering that my despoiler, guardian, judge, advocate, and jury is the British nation itself?

"Generous and Christian Englishmen, accord me a just and liberal treatment for the sake of the fair name of your nation, of which I have now the honour to be a naturalised member, for it is more blessed to give than to take.

"I have the honour to remain, Sir, your most obliged servant,

"DULEEP SINGH.

"Elvedon Hall, Thetford, Suffolk, Aug. 28."

THE TIMES, *Thursday, August* 31, 1882.

"We print elsewhere a somewhat singular letter from the Maharajah Dhuleep Singh. Encouraged, as it would seem, by the restoration of Cetywayo, he puts forward an impassioned plea for the consideration of his own claims. On a first glance, his letter reads as if he demanded nothing less than to be replaced on the throne of the Punjaub. He professes to establish his right to that position and then to waive it, magnanimously avowing that he is quite content to be the subject of his Most Gracious Sovereign, whose graciousness towards him has been boundless. His real object, however, is far less ambitious. It is to prefer a claim for a more generous treatment of his private affairs at the hands of the Indian Government. In lieu of the Sovereignty of the Punjaub, with its unbounded power and unlimited resources, 'the enormous British liberality', he complains, permits him only a life stipend of £25,000 per annum, which is reduced by certain charges to some £13,000. All that he has hitherto succeeded in obtaining from the Indian Government is an arrangement, lately sanctioned by Act of Parliament, whereby he will receive an addition of £2,000 to his annual income, on condition that his estates are sold at his death, in order to liquidate his liabilities, and provide for his widow and children. It is really against this arrangement that the Maharajah appeals. His argument concerning his *de jure* Sovereignty of the Punjaub is manifestly only intended to support his pecuniary claims. If these were settled to his satisfaction, he would doubtless be content, and more than content, to die, as he has lived, an English country gentleman, with estates swarming with game, and with an income sufficient for his needs. This is a sort of appeal to its justice and generosity with which the English public is not unfamiliar. Dhuleep Singh is not the first dispossessed Eastern Prince who has felt himself aggrieved by the dispositions of the Indian Government, nor is this the first occasion on which his own claims have been heard of. For a long time he preferred a claim for the Kohinoor, of which he alleged that he had been wrongfully despoiled. Now, it is his private estates in India which he declares have been confiscated without adequate compensation. No one, of course, would wish that a Prince in the Maharajah's position should be ungenerously treated. He is, as it were, a ward of the English nation, and even his extravagances might be leniently regarded. But as the claim, now publicly preferred by the Maharajah, has been disallowed, after full consideration, by successive Governments, both in India and this country, it may not be amiss to show that his case is by no means so strong as he still affects to consider it.

"The events of two Sikh wars, and their sequel, have probably faded out of the memory of most of our readers. They are, however, accurately stated, so far as the main facts are concerned, in the Maharajah's letter. It is not so much with these facts as with the Maharajah's inferences from them, and with certain other facts which he has not found it convenient to state. It is perfectly true that, after the overthrow of 'Khalsa' power in the sanguinary battle of Sobraon, Lord Hardinge declined to annex the Punjaub, and replaced the Maharajah on the throne under the Regency of his mother, the Ranee, assisted by a Council of Sirdars. This settlement, however, proved a failure, and was replaced by the arrangement made under the Bhyrowal Treaty, whereby the entire control and guidance of affairs was vested in the British Resident, and the presence of British troops was guaranteed until the Maharajah should attain his majority. The second Sikh war, which began with the revolt of Moolraj in 1848, soon proved the futility of this arrangement also; and after the surrender of Mooltan and the battle of Guzerat, which finally broke the reviving power of the Khalsa, Lord Dalhousie, who had succeeded Lord Hardinge as Governor-General, decided that the time had come for the incorporation of the Punjaub with the British Dominions in India. Dhuleep Singh was at this time only eleven years of age, but he had been recognised for more than three years as the Sovereign of the Punjaub, and by the advice of his Durbar at Lahore he signed the terms of settlement proposed by the British Commissioner, whereby he renounced 'for himself, his heirs, and his successors, all right, title, and claim to the Sovereignty of the Punjaub, or to any sovereign power whatever.' By subsequent clauses of the same instrument 'all the property of the State, of whatever description, and wheresoever found', was confiscated to the East India Company; the Kohinoor was surrendered to the Queen of England; a pension of not less than four, and not exceeding five, lakhs of rupees was secured to the Maharajah 'for the support of himself, his relatives, and the servants of the State'; and the Company undertook to treat the Maharajah with respect and honour, and to allow him to retain the title of 'Maharajah Dhuleep Singh, Bahadoor'. Of this instrument, the Maharajah now says that he was compelled to sign it by his guardians when he was a minor, and he argues that the political necessity which dictated it was due to the *lâches* of the Indian Government, which had failed to fulfil the pledges of the Bhyrowal Treaty, and had allowed the revolt of Moolraj to develop into a Sikh rebellion.

"In answer to these allegations, it is sufficient to quote the Report of the British Commissioner who presented the terms for signature. 'The paper,' he says, 'was then handed to the Maharajah, who immediately affixed his signature. The alacrity with which he took the papers when offered was a matter of remark to all, and suggested the idea that possibly he had been instructed by his advisers that any show of hesitation might lead to the substitution of terms less favourable than those which he had been offered.' Moreover, the plea that the Maharajah was a minor, and therefore not a free agent, is fatal to his own case; he was two years younger when the Bhyrowal Treaty was signed, and younger still when the settlement of Lord Hardinge replaced him on the throne, and restored to him the Sovereignty which he even now acknowledges might at that time have been rightly forfeited. We need not dwell on this point, however. The Maharajah himself would hardly press it. His claim of Sovereignty is merely intended to cover his claim for money. He never was much more than nominal Sovereign of the Punjaub, and he probably desires nothing so little at this moment as the restitution of his sovereign rights. The political question has long been closed; it only remains to consider whether the personal and financial question still remains open. The Maharajah complains that he was deprived of his personal and private property—with insignificant exceptions—and of the rentals of his landed estates. There is, however, no mention of private property in the terms of settlement accepted by the Maharajah, and a minute of Lord Dalhousie recorded in 1855, states explicitly that at the time the Punjaub was annexed the youth had no territories, no lands, no property, to which he could succeed. The pension accorded by the East India Company was plainly intended to support the Maharajah in becoming state, and to provide for his personal dependents, and the British Government expressly reserved to itself the right of allotting only such portion as it thought fit of the 'Four Lakh Fund', as the pension was called, to the Maharajah's personal use. So long ago as 1853, Lord Dalhousie wrote a despatch intended to remove from the Maharajah's mind all idea that the Four Lakh Fund would ultimately revert to himself, and characterising such an idea as 'entirely erroneous'.

"The Indian Government, however, has certainly not dealt ungenerously with the Maharajah. It is true that it has not recognised his claim to certain private estates no record of which exists, still less has it listened to any of his attempts to assail the validity of the instrument whereby his sovereignty was extinguished. For some years after the annexation his personal allowance out of the Four Lakh Fund was fixed at £12,500 a year—a sum which was considered entirely satisfactory by the leading Ministers of the Durbar which assented and advised the Maharajah to assent to the terms of 1849. But in 1859 this allowance was doubled, and the Maharajah himself more than once acknowledged, in subsequent years, the liberality of the arrangements made. The allowance of £25,000 a year has been reduced to the £13,000 mentioned by the Maharajah in his letter, not by any act of the Indian Government, but by what, if he were only an English country gentlemen, we should be compelled to call extravagance, though as he is an Eastern Prince it is more generous, perhaps, to describe it as magnificence. He first bought a property in Gloucestershire, but this was sold some years ago, and his present estate at Elveden, in Suffolk, was purchased for £138,000, the money being advanced by the Government, and interest for the loan to the amount of £5,664 per annum being paid by the Maharajah. Some two or three years ago the Home Government of India proposed to release the Maharajah from payment of this annual sum provided that he would consent to the sale of the estate, either at once or at his death, for the repayment of the principal of the loans advanced. This proposal, however, was rejected by the Indian Government, which maintained in very strong and plain language that the Maharajah had already been treated with exceptional liberality and that if he wanted more money he should sell his estate. The Indian Government remained inexorable, but the liberality of the Home Government was not yet exhausted.

The Maharajah had built a house at Elveden at a cost of £60,000, and had borrowed £40,000 from a London banking firm for the purpose. For this loan £2,000 interest had to be paid, and the India Office has lately sanctioned the repayment of the capital sum without making any further charge on the Maharajah. It is to this arrangement, and to the Act of Parliament which sanctions it, that the Maharajah refers with some bitterness at the close of his letter. In order to settle his affairs and to provide for his wife and family, the Act of Parliament requires that his estate at Elveden should be sold after his death. *Hinc illæ lacrymæ.* An argument, which starts from the sovereign claims of the son of the 'Lion of the Punjaub', ends somewhat ridiculously, though not without a touch of pathos, with the sorrows of the Squire of Elveden. Duleep Singh began life as the Maharajah of the Punjaub, with absolute power and boundless wealth, if he had only been old enough to enjoy them, and if the Khalsa would only have allowed him to do so; he is not even allowed to end it as an English country gentlemen, leaving an encumbered estate and an embarrassed heir. There is really a certain tragedy about the whole matter. Fate and the British Power have deprived the Maharajah of the Sovereignty to which he was born. He has done his best to become an English squire, and if he has lived beyond his income he may plead abundance of examples in the class to which he has attached himself; yet he is forced to bear the consequences himself, and not to inflict them on his children and descendants, as an English squire would be able to do. The whole case is one which it is very difficult to judge upon any abstract principles. It is no doubt the duty of every man to live within his income, and yet, if the Maharajah had failed to acquire a virtue rare indeed among Eastern Princes, and not too common in the class to which he belongs by adoption, there is no Englishman but would feel ashamed if he or his descendants were thereby to come to want. At the same time it is impossible for the Indian Government, which has claims on its slender resources far more urgent than those of the magnificent squire of Elveden, to guarantee him indefinitely against the consequences of his own improvidence. At any rate, it is safe to warn him against encumbering his personal claims by political pleas which are wholly inadmissible. He is very little likely to excite sympathy for his pecuniary troubles by his bold, but scarcely successful, attempt to show that if he could only come by his own he is still the lawful Sovereign of the Punjaub."

THE TIMES, *Friday, September* 8, 1882.

"THE CLAIMS OF THE MAHARAJAH DULEEP SINGH.

"TO THE EDITOR OF THE TIMES.

"SIR,—As your leading article of Thursday, the 31st ult., commenting on my letter of the 28th, which you were so good as to publish, contains many inaccuracies as to matters of fact, which no one, perhaps, can correct so precisely as myself, I trust you will allow me to do so, and to make a few observations.

"1. You say: 'All that he has hitherto succeeded in obtaining from the Indian Government is an arrangement, lately sanctioned by Act of Parliament, whereby he will receive an addition of £2,000 to his annual income on condition that his estates are sold at his death, in order to liquidate his liabilities and provide for his widow and children. It is really against this arrangement that the Maharajah appeals.'

"I do not really appeal against the above arrangement, but what I do certainly think unjust in it is that I am not permitted to repay during my life the loan which is to be made under it—£16,000 having already been advanced to me—and that I am thus forbidden to preserve, by a personal sacrifice, their English home to my descendants. In last April I sent a cheque for £3,543 14*s*., representing capital and compound interest at the rate of 5 per cent. to the India Office, but it was returned to me.

"My widow and children, should I leave any, were already provided for under arrangements which existed before this Act was passed.

"2. With reference to your quotation from the British Commissioner as to my 'alacrity' in signing the terms, I have simply to say that, being then a child, I did not understand what I was signing.

"3. 'Moreover,' you say, 'the plea that the Maharajah was a minor, and, therefore, not a free agent, is fatal to his own case; he was two years younger when the Bhyrowal Treaty was signed, and younger still when the settlement of Lord Hardinge replaced him on the throne, and restored to him the sovereignty which he even now acknowledges might at that time have been rightly forfeited. We need not dwell on this point, however. The Maharajah himself would hardly press it.'

"But, whether it is fatal to my case or not, I do press it, and maintain that after the ratification of the Bhyrowal Treaty I was a ward of the British nation, and that it was unjust on the part of the guardian to deprive me of my kingdom in consequence of a failure in the guardianship.

"Here are Lord Hardinge's own words: 'But, in addition to these considerations of a political nature, the Governor-General is bound to be guided by the obligations whioh the British Government has contracted when it consented to be the guardian of the young Prince during his minority.'—(*Vide* page 49, *Punjaub Papers*, 1847-49.)

"4. 'The Maharajah complains,' you would say, 'that he was deprived of his personal and private property—with insignificant exceptions—and of the rentals of his landed estates. There is, however, no mention of private property in the terms of settlement accepted by the Maharajah, and a minute of Lord Dalhousie, recorded in 1855, states explicitly that at the time the Punjaub was annexed the youth had no territories, no lands, no property, to which he could succeed.' My reply is that, at the time of the annexation, I had succeeded to territories, lands, and personal property, and was in possession, and these possessions were held in trust and managed for me, under treaty, by the British Government.

"That I had succeeded and was possessed of privat eestates in land is a historical fact and a matter of public record. Moreover, these estates had belonged to my family, one of them having been acquired by marriage, before my father attained to sovereignty. The statement in Lord Dalhousie's minute only amounts to a denial of the existence of the sun by a blind man; and there are none so blind as those who will not see.

"And now, with regard to my alleged extravagance; these are the facts. The life stipend of £25,000 allotted to me has to bear the following deductions:—(1) £5,664 interest payable to the Government of India; (2) about £3,000 as premium on policies of insurance on my life, executed in order to add to the meagre provision made for my descendants by the British Government and as security for the loan from my bankers; (3) £1,000 per annum for two pensions of £500 per annum each, to the widows of the superintendent appointed by Lord Dalhousie to take charge of me after the annexation, and of my kind friend, the late controller of my establishment, besides which there is some £300 per annum payable in pensions to old servants in India.

"In order to be able to receive His Royal Highness the Prince of Wales, and to return the hospitality of men of my own position in life, and because I was advised, and considered, not, I think, unreasonably, that the rank granted to me by Her Majesty required it to be done, I expended some £22,000—not £60,000, as you were informed—in alterations and repairs to the old house on this estate; suitable furniture cost £8,000 more.

"At a cost of some £3,000 I have purchased life annuities to be paid to the before-mentioned widow ladies, in case they should survive me.

"About £8,000 more had to be borrowed from my bankers on mortgage, to complete the purchase of this estate, as the money lent to me by the Government of India was insufficient by that amount. Thus my debts amount to something like £44,000, of which £30,000 is covered by policies of insurance, £8,000 by mortgage, and the remainder amply secured by personal assets. Therefore, instead of my estates being heavily encumbered, my heirs, if I were to die at this moment, would succeed to a house and furniture, which are worth much more than £30,000, without any liability, besides some £70,000 secured by insurance on my life.

"I think you are bound to acquit the Squire of Elveden of extravagance.

"When the agricultural depression set in I requested the Home Government to make an allowance that would enable me to maintain my position, and they kindly, after causing all my accounts to be examined, helped me with £10,000, but did not accuse me of extravagance. Subsequently, pending the consideration of my affairs, some £6,000 or £7,000 more was advanced to pay off pressing bills, as during that time I had not completed the arrangements for reducing my establishment. Out of the above loan about £10,000 was invested in live and dead stock on farms in hand, and would be forthcoming, if demanded, at a very short notice.

"Thus the extravagance during my residence at Elveden is reduced to the fabulous sum of some £12,000, and I possess enough personalty, beyond any question, to discharge debts to that amount, and some £6,000 more, should they exist at my death.

"In common justice, therefore, Mr. Editor, I ask you to enable me to contradict, in as prominent a manner as they were brought forward in your most influential journal, the rumours as to my extravagance.

"In the first paragraph of your leading article of Thursday, the 31st ultimo, you say that 'the claim now publicly preferred by the Maharajah has been disallowed after full consideration by successive Governments, both in India and this country.' Yes—it is very easy to disallow a claim without hearing the real claimant.

"The English law grants the accused the chance of proving himself not guilty, but I am condemned unheard: is this just?

"I remain, Sir, your most obliged,

"DULEEP SINGH."

"Elveden Hall, Thetford, Suffolk, Sept. 6th."

POSTSCRIPT.

EVEN under the cloud of vituperation with which Lord Dalhousie tried to mystify what he called the "conquest" of the Punjaub, the nature of the transaction must soon have become unpleasantly manifest throughout India, but for the decent covering provided by the "Terms" of 1849, imposed upon the Maharajah Duleep Singh, himself a minor, through the formal act and deed of his Council of Regency. Hardly a show of negotiation or discussion was permitted. Their signatures were extorted from the Councillors, whose conduct throughout the rebellion had been irreproachable, by threats that if they refused to sign, their landed estates would be confiscated, and the Maharajah and themselves would be left to the Governor-General's "mercy", as persons entitled to no "allowance whatever", and to no "consideration". Sir Henry Elliot, who was the British Commissioner on the occasion, writes as follows :—

'The Dewan," Rajah Deena Nath, "who was much more deliberate and reserved than his colleague," Rajah Tej Singh, "commented on the severity of the conditions."

"I replied that, if they refused to accept the terms which the Governor-General offered, the Maharajah and themselves would be entirely at his mercy, and I had no authority to say that they would be entitled to receive any allowance whatever."

"If they did not subscribe to the conditions, I could not promise that any consideration would be shown to them."

"After much more parley, during which I convinced them of my resolute determination to yield no point, they expressed their willingness to sign the Paper, and signed it accordingly, not without evident sorrow and repugnance on the part of the Dewan."*

Thus the British Commissioner who presented the "Terms" for signature, as also in a passage quoted, with singular misapprehension of its bearings, by the writer of the *Times* article, substantially admits the terror, on behalf of their Prince as well as of their own future, by which the Councillors of Regency were compelled to accede to the "Terms". "The paper," says the Commissioner, "was then handed to the Maharajah, who immediately affixed his signature. The alacrity with which he took the papers when offered was a matter of remark to all, and suggests the idea that

* *Punjaub Papers*, 1849, pp. 649, 650, 653.

possibly he had been instructed by his advisers that any show of hesitation might lead to the substitution of terms less favourable than those which he had been offered."*

"His advisers," as we have just seen, had, in fact, been threatened with "the substitution of terms" amounting to proscription and ruin for themselves and their infant Prince.

As for the demeanour and impressions of the Maharajah himself, and "the alacrity" or levity, with which he "took the papers", and "affixed his signature", it is enough to say that he was a child, eleven years of age, and incapable of forming a judgment in such matters.

Here is the full text of the "Terms", dated the 29th of March 1849, "granted to the Maharajah Duleep Singh", which will be found at p. 653 of the *Punjaub Papers* of 1849; and at pp. 269, 270, vol. ii, of the Collection commonly called Aitchison's *Treaties*:†—

"I. His Highness the Maharajah Duleep Singh shall resign for himself, his heirs, and his successors, all right, title, and claim to the Sovereignty of the Punjaub, or to any Sovereign Power whatever.

"II. All the property of the State, of whatever description, and wheresoever found, shall be confiscated to the Honourable East India Company, in part payment of the debt due by the State of Lahore to the British Government, and of the expenses of the war.

"III. The gem called the Koh-i-noor, which was taken from Shah Shooja-ool-Moolk by Maharajah Runjeet Singh, shall be surrendered by the Maharajah of Lahore to the Queen of England.

"IV. His Highness Duleep Singh shall receive, from the Honourable East India Company, for the support of himself, his relatives, and the servants of the State, a pension not less than four, and not exceeding five, lakhs of Company's Rupees per annum.

"V. His Highness shall be treated with respect and honour. He shall retain the title of Maharajah Duleep Singh Bahadoor; and he shall continue to receive, during his life, such portion of the above-named pension as may be allotted to himself personally, provided he shall remain obedient to the British Government, and shall reside at such place as the Governor-General of India may select."

The British Government remained Guardian of the Maharajah after the annexation; and, since he attained his majority, as before, has always exercised the right of interpreting the "Terms", and of allotting the pension prescribed by Article IV. Assuming that the assertion of this right is quite legitimate, and actually unavoidable, it still ought to be exercised with a sense of honourable responsibility, and cannot fairly be exempt from reasonable inquiry and becoming representations by the other party, the Maharajah Duleep Singh, who signed the Terms of 1849. The Maharajah is

* *Ante*, p. 98, *Punjaub Papers*, 1849, p. 652.

† Calcutta, 1863. London: Longmans and Co.

entitled and bound in honour and in duty to plead on behalf of his own interests under that instrument, the Terms of 1849, and on behalf, likewise, of those for whom as well as for himself he was made to sign,—" his heirs and successors".

Just because no other power could intervene or arbitrate between the parties to the "Terms" of 1849,—just because the Maharajah Duleep Singh was and is the weaker party, unable to resist or to appeal to any external authority,—the British Government was bound, legally and morally, to interpret and execute those Terms with something more than scrupulous integrity. The weaker party is entitled, by accepted maxims of international and common law, to the most liberal interpretation of the engagements in question,—not from any sentimental considerations of pity or generosity, but on the reasonable ground that the stronger party, having been able to do so, must be assumed to have imposed the strictest and most severe terms that were politic and prudent at the time, and cannot be allowed, at any subsequent period of advantage, to enhance their stringency, or to diminish the benefits belonging to the weaker party.

It must not be supposed that the scrupulous administration of the annual "four lakh fund" is here impugned. The present writer has not the data before him. It would probably require the services of a competent accountant or actuary to settle whether the Maharajah Duleep Singh has duly "received", in annual payments or special grants, "for himself, his relatives and the servants of the State", the maximum or the minimum amount prescribed by Article IV of the Terms. Sir John Kaye, than whom no one could be better informed, while his language must have been somewhat restrained or chastened by his employment at the India Office, says:—

"The British Government bound themselves to pay the annual sum of forty or fifty thousand pounds to the boy-Prince and his family."

And he adds in a note;—

"This is not the loose diction of doubt. The agreement was that the British Government should pay not less than four, or more than five lakhs of rupees."*

The writer of the article in the *Times* raises the question of the Maharajah's private and personal estate. Misapprehending once more, as it seems to me, the true bearings of his own argument, he says that "there is no mention of private property in the terms of settlement accepted by the Maharajah." Exactly,—"all the property of the State" is mentioned, and is "confiscated"; the Koh-i-noor is mentioned, and "is surrendered"; if had been intended to exact any more private property, real or personal, it ought to

* Kaye's *Sepoy War*, vol. i, p. 47.

have been mentioned in the terms of settlement. But "there is no mention of private property."

Without a careful examination of public records, the details of the real and personal property, to which the Maharajah had succeeded, and which was in the custody of his Guardian when the Terms were signed, and its disposal after the annexation, cannot be traced.

The Maharajah Duleep Singh asserts in his letters to the *Times*, that although his private property is not confiscated under "the Terms", he has been prevented from receiving the rentals of the landed estates to which he had succeeded, which belonged to his family before his father attained to Sovereignty, and which were in his possession under British Guardianship in 1849.* He also states that although, under the "Terms" of 1849, the personal property which he had inherited, and which was in his possession, under British Guardianship, is not confiscated, his jewels and plate, valued at about £250,000, were actually seized in the Palace at Lahore, and given as prize-money to our troops.†

There certainly is not, as the writer in the *Times* observes, any mention of private property in the "Terms". There is, therefore, no confiscation of private property. "All property of the State, of whatever description", having been confiscated by Article II, the Maharajah, under Article III, personally "surrendered" to the Queen of England "the gem called the Koh-i-noor." It is not confiscated, but is given, by the Maharajah personally, to the Queen in person. If this gem had been the "property of the State" it would have been confiscated under Article II.

In 1849, besides the Koh-i-noor, the Maharajah Duleep Singh was in possession of many other gems, which he did not "surrender". The Koh-i-noor was one article in a large collection of jewels, valued, without that unrivalled gem, at something like £250,000. The contents of the jewel-room were not State property, or they would, including the Koh-i-noor, have been confiscated under Article II. They were not surrendered by the Maharajah Duleep Singh, but they were seized by the Government of India.

If the Maharajah's personal assent or authority was required for the surrender and assignment of the Koh-i-noor, it must have been also required for the assignment of the remaining jewels and personal property. But no such assent or authority was given. Therefore the appropriation of the Maharajah's personal property by Lord Dalhousie was entirely unauthorised and unwarrantable.

The fact that the contents of the jewel-room were known to be the Maharajah's private property and not State property, is furthermore proved by Lord Dalhousie having taken upon himself, in the arbitrary process of distribution, to allow the Maharajah

* *Ante*, pp. 95, 101, 102. † *Ante*, pp. 93, 95, 101.

Duleep Singh to retain about a twelfth part of the Palace jewels, valued at about £20,000, for his own use.* These jewels were certainly not presented to His Highness as a gift; they were simply left in his possession.

What, then, became of the rest of the jewels which were taken out of his possession? It is understood that they were thrown into a Prize Fund for the troops engaged in the Punjaub campaign. If so, it was a flagrant malversation of property; for, whether considered as public or private, the contents of the Palace jewel-room could not possibly come under the head of lawful Prize. The Prize or booty of an army is property taken from an enemy in some operation of war, as on the field of battle, or in the storm of a town. There was no fighting in or near the city of Lahore. The Maharajah Duleep Singh was not an enemy. He was the Ally and Ward of the British Government, and was so proclaimed and upheld throughout the rebellion. His Palace, his possessions, and his person had been for three years in charge of the British Resident at Lahore, and so continued until the date of the "Terms" of 1849.

If these things be so, it would certainly seem that, over and above and beyond the demands avowed in the Terms of 1849, Lord Dalhousie, immediately after their conclusion, enforced certain exactions at the expense and to the detriment of the Maharajah Duleep Singh, which were not imposed or sanctioned by those Terms.

If these things be so, whatever might have been his position, had he and his advisers been exposed to the "mercy" of Lord Dalhousie by any want of "alacrity" in signing the Terms of 1849,† the Maharajah Duleep Singh, appealing to these Terms, is in the position of a person with whom a bargain was made, and from whom much more than the proper proceeds of that bargain have been extorted. And his position, on legal and moral principles, is not weaker but stronger, because, at the time of the bargain being made, he was an infant and the weaker party, nor because the stronger party, at the time of the bargain being made, and for several subsequent years, was the infant's Guardian and Trustee.

* *Ante*, p. 95. † *Ante*, p. 101.